One More Time

By **DON MUSGRAVES**

With **Dave Balsiger**

bethany
fellowship

Minneapolis, Minnesota

Library of Congress Cataloging in Publication Data

Musgraves, Don, 1935-
One More Time.
1. Alcoholics—Personal narratives.
I. Balsiger, Dave.
II. Title.
HV5293.M87A35
362.2'92'0924 [B]
74-1395

Published by Bethany Fellowship, Inc.
6820 Auto Club Road, Minneapolis, Minnesota 55438

Printed in the United States of America

DEDICATED TO

My wife, Loris,
whose deep and abiding faith in God
sustained our lives
when I had no faith in anything

Rejoice not against me, O mine enemy:
when I fall, I shall arise . . .

Micah 7:8

Foreword

I have been asked to write a foreword to this book, not because of an extensive, long-standing acquaintance with the author, but because of a long-term commitment to and involvement in the ministry to men with problems and attitudes similar to Don's.

In sharing details of his own spiritual pilgrimage, Don Musgraves has attempted to reveal the complexity of the human dilemma. He has tried to project the agony and frustration that characterize the life orbiting around itself. It is the common symptom of the unredeemed human nature.

He has related the dramatic and dynamic change that Christ makes in a life that opens to Him as Lord. That change is even noticeable in the flow and style of the writing as the events of God's will begin to unfold in Don's life.

The ministry and work to which Don has now dedicated his life is how I first met him. He brought music groups to the institution in California where I was serving as chaplain. He molded their presentation around the existing ministry and program, thus supporting and enhancing it. That is a significant feature of his work.

What Don has been he is now letting God take and work together for good, using his past as a resource for his ministry to those who are still in need of God's deliverance, and a source of encouragement to those who have already experienced it.

If this book succeeds in opening the hearts of people to care about persons in institutions, and helps to open doors of institutions to those caring people, it will have accomplished the mission to which I am sure it is dedicated. That mission I see expressed in 2 Corinthians 5: 17-20.

Austin L. Ingram
Protestant Chaplain
Federal Correctional Institution
Texarkana, Texas

Preface

Most of my life I have had the desire to be a genuine person with a definite self-identity. During that same period of time, I always fell short of my idealistic goal and lived behind facades and philosophies which never satisfied my ambition for purposeful self-identity.

Driven by this identity quest, I soared to a successful apex in my career only to tumble back into the deepest despair of failure. My actions over several years caused my parents, my family, my employers, and myself to suffer great social and mental anguish.

The door to recovery was finally exposed to me as a great miracle—a personal relationship with Jesus Christ.

I knew I needed a miracle long before I met the Lord. This is also the testimony of most of the "down and outers" I have met along the way—in jails, mental wards, bars, and on the streets.

Jesus Christ can make a new person out of anyone, and *One More Time* is the story of how it's done!

—Don Musgraves

Acknowledgements

Neither this book nor Chrisma Ministries, Inc. would have been possible without the prayer, fellowship, teaching, advice, or assistance of the following people: My wife, Loris; my mother, Ruby Irene; my grandmother, Jettie Ogletree; my children, Mike, Lynne and Tracy; Dave and Janie Balsiger, Les and Sally Jones, David and Gwen Medina, Frank and Sue Morton, Gene and Shirley Browning, George and Betty Wakeling, Steve and Charla Koska, Pastor Ralph Wilkerson, Dick and Barbara Simmons, Gary and Cindy Reynolds, Julia Taylor, Chaplain Jene Firth, and the fantastic staff at Melodyland Hotline Center.

Table of Contents

Chapter 1

When the judge on the cold January day said that all the time I had to spend behind bars was six months for writing bad checks, that judge was anticipating Valentine's Day. I couldn't believe it.

But as I lay on my sagging bunk with my eyes shut against the dinginess of my cell, I would be on Cloud Nine thinking how sweet that judge was, then I would drop right back to earth thinking of all the time that hadn't been mentioned on the other charges. This yo-yoing of my feelings was the story of my life.

"Come off it, Don," I told myself. "Don't go soft in the head. You're only talking about one count—one out of five. How about the FBI deal, just for starters? You could build some time in a federal pen for that—after your lease here is expired, that is."

Here was the Orange County Jail, Santa Ana, in Southern California. It had been constructed in the Stone Age. Thirty years ago, they'd condemned it, they'd forgotten it. The building had been intended to serve a sleepy little community lost in orange groves.

Out of a suspended two years on a check rap, I had served one of six months. Not tried yet was nonsupport, violation of a five-year probation, transporting a stolen vehicle across a state line in defiance of the Dyer Act (a federal deal), and defrauding an innkeeper.

I could get sixty years.

"You got a letter, Musgraves," Sammy growled,

13

"from your old lady." He had already examined the envelope, back and front, with cold steel eyes, squinting at the blurred postmark.

Custody had elected Sammy dictator, after he had put himself up for nomination with his fists. Number One in each cell block was the guy who could back up his hard talk with muscles and guts.

The guards? Why should they care what we did to amuse ourselves? It was convenient for them to take advantage of Sammy's willingness to handle petty details. He could get away with a lot more rough stuff than they, and when a guard needed the men lined up smartly, Sammy did the job.

Another valentine, perhaps? I hadn't expected my wife to answer. In my letter to her, I'd told her I *realized* I was a creep. . . .

"Loris," I had written, "I know I've put you through hell. . . . I've always loved you . . . needed you terribly. I'll never give up trying to find a way for us to be a family. If you decide you don't want to answer this letter, I won't blame you—and I won't bother you with any more. Just remember one thing: So far I don't know of any rule that says that two people in our circumstance have to stay this way forever—and no one has the right to make rules for another human being that say, 'That's it. You're not allowed to try anymore.'" I had signed it *Don*, along with my number, 46488.

Now as I looked at the envelope, surprised and heartened that she had answered me, I was aware of the others staring at me. I tore at the envelope.

After a few words, I wished I had waited to read it when I had a couple of minutes alone. Only Sammy could have been totally without sympathy seeing the hurt that must have shown on my face.

Hurt? I'd earned it, and more, just as I had earned those six months and, if it came to that, the sixty years. Still, it *hurt*.

Loris had written:

Dear Don,

I received your letter today. After reading it, I can't help but compare it with all of the other letters you've written while you were locked up some place. They're all so very much alike. They all say the very same thing. I know at this moment you have good intentions, but you always did before, too, and look at what happened.

As for your "just reward," I don't think there is any justice, not when someone like you is allowed to run around loose and, as for your six months' sentence, I wish it had been six years.

It's ironic, isn't it, that the man I loved so much, the man who taught me how to love, is now the object of all my hate. You once told me there was a very fine line between love and hate. You were so right. I could never in a million years convey to you the hurt and frustration and the humiliation you've caused me—and I know if I let you, you'd go right on taking advantage of me forever. Well, I never intend to let you in any way ever hurt or degrade or humiliate me again. You're never going to have another chance to walk out on me or the children again.

You will never know the harm you've done to Mike. No one knows but me. I'm the one who has to answer his questions about you, and I'm the one who hears him crying for his daddy. He doesn't think he'll ever see you again. It breaks my heart. It is so unfair. I cannot understand why little children should have to suffer for something which isn't their fault. I think I hate you more than anything else because of what all this has done to Mike. If he were older I could tell him simply that his father was a drunk and that would be that. But he's still just a little boy and has to be protected. Have you ever stopped to think of what will happen in a few years? One day soon Mike will be old enough to figure everything out for himself. And, then, what about Lynne, when she is old enough?

Drunk after drunk, and jail after jail, and woman after woman, you keep telling me you love me. Do you really expect me to believe you? How could you possibly love me and still continue to live the way you do and do the ridiculous things you do? And, as for needing me, do you think you're the only one in the world who needs someone? I've always needed you. You seem to think that I'm made out of stone, that no matter what happens, I'll come through unscarred and unaffected. I think the reason you've always needed me so

15

much is because you are a thoroughly selfish person and so very weak.

You seem to think that you can draw strength from me, but you can't. It doesn't work that way. You are responsible for what you are and for all of your actions. If you are ever going to change, you're going to have to rely on yourself, not me. I can't help you and neither can your precious bottle.

You're perfectly welcome to correspond with the children. They need the reassurance that they still have a father and that he still loves and cares about them— but remember one thing: they are still too little to be told where you are or what you've done. And don't write anything derogatory about yourself. No one has ever said anything to them about where you've been all these months. They've just assumed that you've been far away somewhere working.

Monday I have to make another trip to the District Attorney's office. As long as you're in jail, I think I can draw so much a month. Any little bit will help.

I wish there was something I could say that would make you feel like the heel you are, but then I guess you know better than anyone else what you are. I only hope that every day of your confinement is like an eternity and every night one long continuous nightmare.

Loris

Chapter 2

What was I doing here anyway? What was my excuse for being penned up with these failures, drifters from one drunk to the other, from one mugging to the next? What was I doing associating with these pushers, stick-up men, car thieves?

Many of these foul-mouthed and violent men had never known a happy home. They might as well have been born in the Orange County Jail. Some had had mothers who could only guess what men might have gotten them into trouble.

Their fathers, if around, were the kind that blew their paychecks on booze and their time on trivial pursuits in the blues of the night. They beat their wives and exposed their ragged children to words and thoughts gathered in garbage heaps and dark alleys.

Jake was one of these guys. He was only twenty-two years old but he had been in Youth Authority for a total of three years off and on, and real, grown-up *jail* another two, with a promise of promotion to San Quentin.

"Man, when I finish this stretch," Jake said one day while I was mopping the cell block on Sammy's orders, "I'm going to soup up my sports car. Then when I tool up that freeway, I'll leave those cops in Questionville. I've been studying those off-ramps in my spare time here. Now I got the picture, you better believe it. That's how you slip out of a drunk driving rap, when you know your off-ramps."

Rock Baily sneered. "From the way you describe that machine, it's all strung out. . . ."

"Back off, Rocky. Talking about being strung out, when did you have your last fix?"

"Do I look unhappy?" Rock spread his hands. "All you have to have around here is a little *money.* . . ."

Rock was one of those spoiled fruits of suddenly affluent parents, dads who made the executive scene straight out of college; overripened in the permissive climate of California's sunny, slick society, fed too much on sweets and sweet talk, indulged, catered to, cajoled, and coddled.

"If they was any drugstores in this here jail," Bob said, "I'd do me all right, I bet you. I real good breaking in that's why I wear sneakers for." He shrugged. "I also good in breaking the *guy* if he still in there and don't want to give me no pills." He looked around the cell with his yellow-red eyes. "Like, I could break you jokers if you trouble me, you know?"

So it was . . . some of the inmates rationalized that their skin color made the difference between the in's and the out's; others, their broken homes, their parents, their schools, churches, neighbors, loan counsellors, corner cop, I.Q., mental or physical disabilities, you name it.

All had tailor-made alibis as easy to slip into as a familiar suit, comfortable.

The visitors who looked in on the animals in these cages could cite still more *causes.*

Sociologists, criminologists, and psychologists all have their pet theories. Businessmen, housewives, and politicians can elucidate many reasons for the soaring crime rate and tell you what you have to do to curb it and how to make prisons work. They can tell the wardens a thing or two. Eliminate poverty . . . redistribute the wealth . . . go to church . . . put down organized religion . . . install socialism, communism, dictatorship. Soak the rich . . . bring back free enterprise . . . control population. Support women's liberation . . . abolish the credit system . . . bring back prohibition . . . legalize heroin . . . decentralize industry.

My mind whirled as I went over the contents of Loris' letter and for the zillionth time asked myself, "Why am *I* here?" I was at a loss to account for my bizarre behavior, the incredible things I had done. I wasn't even a rebel.

I had been neither wealthy nor extremely poor; though during the depression as a boy, I had helped my family pick cotton until my father, along with the nation, recovered. I didn't come from a broken or unhappy home, and I wasn't an only child; neither was I lost in a crowd of siblings.

I was above average in intelligence but not a precocious genius resentful of "dead level" democracy.

Then . . . why?

I lay awake that night, tortured, weeping, looking back over my life, trying to answer this unanswerable question, to piece together the enigmatic jigsaw.

Why was I such a monstrous creep?

Chapter 3

Sixteen! For some reason, my sixteenth birthday party in Oklahoma kept coming back as I lay on my bunk.

"Happy birthday to you, happy birthday to you . . . ," everyone sang. Dad's voice stood out from the others.

"Hey Don," Dean said, "how does it feel to be sixteen? I'd have gotten you a razor, only I didn't think you were ready for it. Well, go on. Open your presents." Dean was only thirteen then, and he had a comment for everything.

On the table next to the cake lay a small box. I suspected the key to a lot of happiness was in there.

I left the small package until last, thanking my brothers, and Gramps and Grandma, for their presents. When I picked up the box, Dean let out a whistle.

The white box contained a key—to a 1947 Chevie.

"I've signed for it, Don," Dad said. "All you have to do is pay for it."

Everyone laughed. We all knew Dad meant it. He hadn't been a used car dealer for the past four years for nothing. He had the reputation of being honest—too honest—but his friends said he had never lost money on a deal yet. Since junior high school days and a paper route, I had had jobs and had earned money. I wasn't worried.

When I started Capitol Hill High School in Oklahoma City, there were over 4,000 students to compete with, and I was determined to make a name for myself. I had heard the way to get "into things" was to be in one of the pep clubs. I joined one, and in my first year I was elected secretary of the Redskins, one of the best of the clubs. Another "must" for top man was to have a car. This key, then, meant a lot more than my parents could guess. It opened the door to prestige, scoring with girls, and being popular with the "upper crust"—the future executive set.

"This has really been some birthday!" I managed to say as the whole family crowded into the car and Dad sat next to me, as he had when first teaching me to drive.

"Take it out on the highway, Don," Dean pleaded. "Let's see if it's got any guts."

"Don! Take it easy!" Mom gasped.

The wheel responded to the lightest touch as I turned out onto the main highway, putting my foot down on the accelerator, playing with it to get the feel.

The car picked up fast. I looked at Dad. "You weren't kidding, were you? This motor is really hot!"

As I drove along through the country, I could feel that certain closeness which sometimes bound our family together. I guess it had started before I was born when Dad, Mom, and my grandmother had driven clear out to Ducor, California, during the depression in the 1930s to pick cotton together, not satisfied to stand in the bread lines or take a handout.

I could hardly wait to get to school the next morning to show off.

"Hey, Don, give us a lift in your new wheels," Pat called the minute I drove up. He and four other guys piled in and we gave it a real test out back of the school.

"How you going to pay for this? I didn't know you'd been putting any money away, the way you're such a big spender," Pat said. He had had to work hard for his car and he had warned me how much it cost for gasoline, insurance, and upkeep.

I had been told that money can't buy happiness but, as a teenager, I didn't believe it. Most stupid thing I ever heard, I thought. Everything I wanted cost money: dates, hamburgers, cokes, clothes. Everything!

"What do you mean, how am I going to pay for this?"

21

I answered. "I work for my money, same as you guys."

From then on, I thought I had it made. I was going steady with a popular girl, I was in clubs like the de Molay and the Pep Club, had a good car, a job, and enough money to keep up with the other kids.

In giving me the car, my parents thought they were helping me. At that time, I heartily agreed. As it turned out, that car got me started on a downhill trip. It opened up a new world to me—an underworld of self-indulgence, pursuit of pleasure, waste.

One Saturday, three of my friends—Bob, Don, and Pat—piled into the car with me and we all took off looking for excitement.

As we drove past a grocery store, Bob yelled, "Stop, Don! Let's go see if we can get some beer."

We sat in the car planning how we would go about it. Then we walked nonchalantly into the store, picked out eight-quart bottles of Carling's Black Label Beer, put them on the check stand, and waited for the guy to laugh.

Instead, he rang them up and put them in a bag.

We paid and, without looking at each other, left the store, got into the car and took off.

We were almost disappointed that it had been so easy. Something had happened that wasn't supposed to happen, and it had taken a bit of the edge off the thrill. We laughed at our cleverness, however, all the way to Bob's house.

Bob brought out potato chips and nuts, and we sat around in his living room drinking and talking about school, sports, and girls. I hadn't tried alcohol before and soon I started to laugh and giggle, and roll on the floor. It was catching. Everyone followed my lead and we finally lay there just looking up at the ceiling, letting the effects of the alcohol tingle through our bodies. I had never felt such freedom, such exhilaration. I felt now as if Don Musgraves could accomplish anything he set out to do.

I could tell Pat was feeling the same way. We were

very close. In opposing pep clubs and both aiming to be tops in them, we were still good friends.

This wasn't Bob's first drinking experience. He was used to it. He had a better house than most of us. His parents were out of town often, and he had a lot of freedom—too much freedom.

As we lay there on the floor, we vowed to do this again. This was really great. We could use Bob's house whenever his folks were gone; if the coast wasn't clear, we knew we could find another place. We all made a pact that day to stay buddies and not to tell anyone what we did when we were together.

Liquor had opened more doors for me. We alternated the beer with whiskey once in a while, and we all got used to consuming more and more each weekend. The alcohol did something special. My shyness with girls evaporated. The liquor helped me turn from a country bumpkin into one of the big wheels, an easy rider along the date trail.

A group of us would pile into the car and go to one of the dances sponsored by the local Kiwanis Club every Friday night. I became one of the best dancers in the school by my junior year and had my pick of girls. I kept eyeing one in particular—Betty.

Betty was slim, pretty, and vivacious, her darting brown eyes always looking for fun. She had naturally curly brown hair and knew how to dress.

I fell in love with Betty and asked her to go steady with me. I gave her my class ring and asked her to quit dating other guys. She accepted the ring but not the idea of going just with me. But we were intellectually compatible and she liked to do the same things that I did. I thought she was the ideal girl for me.

When I made pep club president, I figured Betty would be impressed. "So?" she said. "Big deal." Then reconsidered. "Of course, I knew you were going to make Redskins' prexy. They couldn't have chosen anyone else."

But Dad really sat up and took notice. Both parents at the dinner table that night were thrilled.

"Hey, Don," Dean piped up. "Isn't your friend Pat the president of that other pep club? You're rivals now, I bet."

"Naw. He was just as flipped out as I was," I answered. "That's better than competing with each other in the *same* club."

Actually, Pat had helped me get into the inner circle at school and always built me up with the gang who really counted. I wanted *in* on everything at that high school. Being an officer in clubs meant that you sat up front at the meetings with everyone looking at you, and also it meant you were hip to what was going on in school. It didn't take long for me to find out that I wanted to be in the center of things. I always picked jobs that would put the spotlight on me. I made sure I had friends in the right places, too.

"If you keep on getting a good education, work hard as you are now, son, you'll be able to write your own ticket," Dad said.

This was the umpteenth time he'd said this.

"Uh, excuse me, folks," I said, squirming. "I'll be late for a very important date if I don't hurry. But thanks loads for the nice dinner, Mom."

The truth of the matter was, I was anxious to meet Pat. We had plans—big plans—for that evening.

"Don't be out too late, son," Mom said. "You've been out so much you're beginning to look kind of beat."

"Well, he's got so many girl friends, he has to date two the same evening," Dean teased.

"Aw, come off it." I blushed. "See ya later."

I barely got out the door before Pat drove up. "Where you been? I buzzed by three times. Having trouble getting out?" Pat shot the question to me as I climbed in and slammed the door.

"Since your battery got ripped off today, why don't we cruise around and see what we can find?"

"Drive on a while then. After a while, we can park and go on foot."

When we came to a remote section of town we parked and started walking. Pat carried his battery strap and I carried a crescent wrench.

It was pitch black. After walking about eight blocks, we spotted a car somewhat like mine. The lights were out on the block and the street deserted. "Geez, these people go to bed with the chickens," I whispered. We started to laugh, then hushed quickly.

"I'll loosen the bolts and hand them to you." Pat raised the hood quietly. "There, now . . . help me lift this bugger out."

We walked a block before saying anything more. We had to resist the urge to laugh out loud at our boldness and the fact that we weren't discovered. "Who said crime doesn't pay?" I asked. "Of course, if some joker hadn't lifted *my* battery, I wouldn't have to resort to such tricks."

As we sauntered along swinging that heavy battery between us, it seemed perfectly natural. It didn't occur to me to ask why it was so easy for me to *steal*. It didn't bother me to put on one face to my parents, another to my accomplice, Pat. Somehow, it didn't occur to me that doing this kind of thing was being dishonest.

Lifting the battery was the heaviest heisting I'd done to date, but not the only example. Some of my friends and I had played little games in dime stores not too long ago, and in markets, too.

I'd never been caught.

"Now, swiping hub caps," I said, "that's a real art. Not a job for butterfingers. You let one of those slip out of your hands, and the whole neighborhood wakes up."

"We're doing okay, so far," Pat said. "Think we'll ever get caught?"

"I doubt it. We're clean-cut, all-American kids. Whatever that is."

We got the battery safely to my family's garage without disturbing my parents and installed it in my car. I thought about the guy who would step on his accelerator in the morning, intending to zoom off to work. I laughed.

The next few months of school were even more interesting.

At home, things got interesting, too. Mom knew of a teenage boy who came from a broken home. She invited him to come live with us. I suppose she figured Dean and I would be a good influence on him.

25

It turned out his name was Don, too, and he had a car just like mine, only a different color. He was a year older, about to graduate, and I really looked up to him.

This other Don knew a few tricks that Pat, Bob, and I didn't, and it wasn't long before all of us were fast friends. One night he suggested that since we both needed tires for our cars, we should pick up some. "You get two, Musgraves, and I get two. A deal?" He looked at Pat and Bob. "You guys will lend a hand, won't you?"

Pat shrugged. "I don't know. It's kind of risky, isn't it? I mean, rolling four tires down the street—?"

"Well, if you two are chicken—" Don Alexander said.

"Aw, heck, Pat," Bob said. "We can tell anyone who wants to know we're being initiated into the Ku Klux Klan, or something."

Around ten o'clock, we started looking around. Up and down streets we cruised, checking out likely cars, inspecting tire treads for size. Then we saw a car under a street lamp—a new car with good looking tires.

We were onto that car like a swarm of bees. Bob worked the jack, I loosened the nuts, and Don and Pat rolled the tires off and onto the guy's lawn so they wouldn't make any noise. One by one, the hub caps would drop into a waiting hand, the nuts twirl off, and a tire leave the wheel.

Each one of us rolled a tire back to my car. It wasn't until we were well out of sight that we uttered a sound. "Well done, boys," Don A. said as he passed a bottle around. "You really got that car in bad shape fast!"

We all guffawed thinking about that guy coming out the next morning and seeing his pride and joy sitting there on its brake drums. It didn't occur to any of us that we were hurting someone. We just knew we needed tires, so we took them.

If any of us had asked my dad, we could have gotten tires very cheaply through his connections in the car business. But it was too much fun this way.

While Dad was always telling me to "work hard, get an education, keep your nose clean," I began to wonder how to stay honest when you have an overwhelming urge to be dishonest.

I began to realize that, at this point in my senior year, I was living several different lives: one at school, one at work, one at home, and one out with the boys at night. My job at the print shop was a separate thing, then. I didn't cheat anybody, fudge on time, or try anything out of line. It meant too much to me to want to take any chances losing it. Why didn't I feel like this about my parents, or the image I was creating with my friends?

By the end of our senior year, we were all big shots at graduation. In a school of that size, we had really made a big splash.

Until I started tramping the streets looking for a good paying job at the age of seventeen, it hadn't dawned on me that I wasn't very well trained for anything in particular.

When I'd been accustomed to being treated like royalty by both teachers and fellow students, going from place to place begging for work got to be pretty demoralizing. Most of the adults in the community were too busy to give me much time. With them, I didn't cut the dashing figure I had at high school. I was just another body sitting in a personnel office.

It was a bitter blow, this reception by the town. Often I washed away the bitterness with a stealthy swig of liquor.

Betty got a job right away, though, in a jewelry store.

To celebrate her achievement, I took her to see "From Here to Eternity," starring hero of the day, Burt Lancaster. The whole Army scene impressed me: the drinking, the illicit love affairs among the officers' wives, the feeling of being a big shot in an officers' club—the whole scene.

I must have nudged Betty a dozen times through that movie, trying to tell her in my own way how moved I was.

I felt her tears dropping on my hand holding hers, and I thought she was as deeply moved as I.

I vowed, then and there, to enlist in the Army. I was sure such a heroic act, which might lead to action in Korea, would impress her.

Possibly this feeling was complemented by the fact

that I was having trouble finding a job, was no longer Mr. It, and several of my friends were enlisting or being drafted.

The longer I thought about it, the stronger was my conviction that without a job, I might lose my car, my friends . . . even Betty.

As things stood now, I was *nobody.*

Chapter 4

In 1953, Joseph Stalin died, Russia dropped its first H-Bomb, the Mau Mau terror raged in Africa, the Korean Armistice had been signed, Edmund Hillary conquered Mount Everest, and Don Musgraves conquered Fort Campbell, Kentucky. I had endured many weeks of rugged training and now stood in formation with other smartly attentive men while two officers went down the line, shaking hands with each man, saying a few words, and then pinning on his bulging chest the coveted wings of the U.S. Army Paratroopers.

Although I had played hard, and had been *drinking* more and more during these wild Army days, I had also *worked* hard for this moment, for this opportunity to show Oklahoma City, Betty Doakes, and everyone else that Don Musgraves was *someone*, after all. Even after they had given the high school hero the cold shoulder the minute he stepped out onto the streets with his diploma.

I had tensed my muscles, gritted my teeth, worked like a slave, and pulled myself back onto the heap, after all!

Oh, I can remember they'd brainwashed us to feel just this way. When Vern Greenwood and I had first talked to the Airborne man at Camp Chaffee, Arkansas, while we were still at the Army Regional Training Base, and told him we wanted to transfer from artillery to Jump School, they had poured it on.

"You'd be taking on a level of training and discipline that no other outfit in the Army demands of you, Musgraves," the officer said. "If you are even selected for training in Kentucky, you'll sweat blood before you even get to jump out of a plane."

I wanted to show Betty Doakes a thing or two. She had played me for a sucker. I had joined the Army in the first place mainly to impress her. I was sure I was in love with her and she had led me to believe she loved me.

I should have come to my senses when she didn't cry at our good-bye. I'd gotten up early, before sun-up, that cold, grey day. Shivering in the bus station, I was already sorry I had signed up. My dad had been opposed to my volunteering for this special two-year hitch, but he didn't get bent out of shape. He shook my hand and said, "Don, keep your nose clean, salute the officers, work hard, and you can write your own ticket."

Mom was really upset. "Be sure to stay warm," she said between tears, "Let us know if you need anything."

"See you," was Betty's good-bye.

It was cold when we arrived at Camp Chaffee—just above freezing. The first morning, we were aroused long before daylight and hustled out to line up at the mess hall—two thousand of us standing in pitch blackness as the wind tore at heavy Army-issue overcoats over our civilian clothes.

It was rugged. Because of my high living, I wasn't in the best physical condition. It was torture getting out of bed, and impossible to stay awake in class.

During all this time, I thought and dreamed about Betty, the excitement I felt parading her around. From that first hour standing in line in the cold darkness, waiting to get breakfast, I'd thought of her.

And during all those early basic training days, body hurting, hustling on the double everywhere, putting in long days in class and on the shooting range I thought of Betty.

I decided to propose. I phoned long distance. "You and I are engaged, baby," I said after a few words. "Okay?" I waited tensely.

Betty was silent for a few seconds. "Well, gee, I guess so," she finally answered.

"I was hoping you'd say that. Listen, honey, I'll make you the best husband there is. Honest. Listen, baby—our time's running out. Since you work in a jewelry store, just pick out an engagement ring. I'll pay for it on installments. Okay?"

"Sure, sweetheart. Uh, what kind of engagement ring? I mean, what do you think . . .?"

"Pick out what really sends you. Don't worry about how much it costs, or anything. I'll pay for it on easy terms. . . . I'll be bucking hard in this man's army and before you know it, I'll make sergeant. I'll be getting leave pretty soon. Uh, I'd better hang up." I started to put the receiver on the hook, then blurted out, "I love you."

After all this buildup, I was out on a limb. I knew I wasn't due for enough time off to get to and from Oklahoma while I was still training.

I approached the commanding officer. "Sir, I need a three-day pass."

The CO snorted. "So do five trillion other recruits."

"I'm going to get married."

He thought it over a minute, all the time staring at me. Finally, he said, "Musgraves. You're a good man. I've had my eye on you. You get along with the other men. You make friends easily. You work hard and you play hard. If you . . ." He opened his desk drawer, pulled out a pad, and began writing. " . . . stay in line, you're going to get some stripes. Ever thought of going to OCS?"

"I'm still thinking about everything, sir," I said. "I haven't really made any decisions."

I didn't have time to call and tell Betty I was coming. When I arrived in Oklahoma City and took a cab to her house, she wasn't home. I waited for her on her porch. I didn't want to do anything else—go anywhere—until I saw her. I was losing my cool. After all, we were engaged. Around one o'clock in the morning, a car braked to a stop in front of her house.

I got up from the porch swing, where Betty and I had sat other times back when. I stood there in the dark, in the shadows, and squinted, trying to make out whose car it was, who was in it. By the street light I could see her and the driver kissing.

She got out, slammed the door and started up the walk toward the house, humming. I met her half way to the house. She had on a low-cut blouse revealing generous hunks of anatomy. The strap of her bra was half down and she was still fingering it as she probably had been doing when she'd been horsing around with her date, knowing full well it attracted his attention all the more.

"So, that's what you've been doing while I've been away," I said.

She started as though she'd seen a ghost. "Don! *Darling*! When did you blow in?"

"Don't change the subject," I sputtered. "Who the hell was that guy? And how come you're going out with guys? And staying out till all hours of the morning? I thought we were engaged?"

"That's a long way from being married, big boy," she purred. She suddenly dodged around me and ran up to the porch.

She couldn't get the door unlocked fast enough; I leaped up the steps, grabbed her and jerked her around to face me. "You're going to listen to me!" I shook her so hard her head jerked from side to side. "Do you know what you've done to me? You're the one I joined the Army for. I thought you'd be proud of me—true to me. What do you want from a guy, anyway? I join the Army and work and suffer to show you how I feel about you, and then you hardly ever write. You could even have visited me . . ."

She winced at my loudness and words.

"You sure exposed yourself tonight," I went on. "Actually, you did me a favor."

"What do you mean—?" She cried and writhed as I held her arms in a vice. "Why didn't you tell me you were coming—?"

"Hah! I'm glad I didn't have a chance to." I grabbed her wrist with one hand and held her hand up to her face, the huge engagement ring almost smashing against her eyeball. "That ring . . . if you want to keep it, you can damned well pay for it yourself. I'm through. Get it? Finished! I wouldn't touch you with a ten-foot pole."

I hurled her away from me so hard she fell back against the door and slid down hard on her seat, back against the screen.

On the way back to camp in the Greyhound bus, I nursed a bottle of whiskey and tried to shake off the hurt and anger I felt. It went deep. This whole Army bit was her fault.

Betty's apparent attraction for me had been the only thing that buoyed me up after graduation. Then, the night of the movie, the feel of her tears on my hand at the dramatic parts had made me think she was capable of feeling deeply. My assumption that joining the Army would make me look good in her eyes had been my salvation.

Then, when she'd consented to marry me . . .

At last! Musgraves amounts to something! Finally, I felt important! *Someone* loves Don Musgraves, after all.

The liquor was getting to me as the Greyhound bus bumped along through the dismal night. Suddenly, I dropped my head onto my chest and sobbed.

When I got back to camp, I hit the bottle. Drunk every night, and on weekends, bombed out of my mind.

It didn't work. I had to figure a way to climb back on top of the heap. I had chosen artillery school as the next step after my eight weeks of basic, but it was no big thing, after all.

Vern Greenwood started Musgraves on the come-back trail as far as status was concerned. Vern and I got acquainted with each other while having lunch one day on the firing range.

During the latter part of our eight weeks of artillery school, Vern and I became great friends and, when we knocked ideas around as to what we wanted to do in the Army, the subject of the Airborne came up. We both agreed *this* would be our cup of tea.

Of course, we had to drink whiskey on it.

We applied, were accepted and presently found ourselves boarding a train for Fort Campbell, Kentucky.

We were going to show the Army a thing or two.

We started out with a big splash. Although opposites in some ways, we both liked to drink but, on the positive side, we were *good* for each other. We made a gentleman's agreement to be the best looking "legs" in the camp. Long before other neophytes got around to understanding paratroopers' *pride*, we were really G.I. We kept our uniforms clean and pressed so the creases were sharp as razor blades. Our boots actually *glowed*.

We played as hard as we worked, which naturally meant we got into scrapes frequently. But we did such a good job while on duty, our superiors liked us and went out of their way to forgive us our trespasses. The most serious disciplinary actions taken were confinement to the base and—push-ups.

Although I escaped more serious punishment, I did talk to a few prisoners in the post stockade, and began to get some idea of the psychology of people who chronically get into trouble. I never dreamed that later I would be just like them! Many had started their downward trend by way of the bottle, but I didn't recognize the warning.

During the week before the wings ceremony, I was looking forward to the big blast, which our officers had promised us, as much as to the ceremony itself. The party was part of the ritual for novice jumpers, and it turned out to be wildly befitting the unique conditions of the Airborne.

Part of the "initiation" was to drink, from the bottom half of a .105 howitzer shell, a witches' brew of six to eight ounces of all kinds of liquor: vodka, rum, whiskey, brandy, and others.

Even this fling wasn't enough to satisfy me. Besides, the fun was dampened by the knowledge that I had guard duty in a few hours. Vern was disappointed. "I've got a pass. I thought you and me could go to my hometown," he said. "You know . . . stop along the way. There's a bunch of little swinging towns between here and there and I know lots of those bartenders personally."

I thought a minute. "Why don't I just take off, anyway? I could tell the CO I got so drunk during *their* celebration I wasn't in control."

We edged out of the recreation hall, picked up Vern's car and hit the road. We stopped at every joint along the way. We told bartenders, and whoever else was near, the story of our accomplishment. Each time, the story was embellished. By the time we arrived at Vern's parents'

34

place, we were jolly jumping giants—and really bombed out.

Sunday night, I had a cool reception from the officer of the day. I did some fast talking and, given my ability to talk my way out of a jam, I managed to put it over. Fortunately, this officer didn't know about my drinking habits, or that my capacity to hold my liquor without getting drunk was way up there.

The net result was that, while I avoided court-martial, I had to spend the next fourteen days confined to the post.

During these fourteen days, I had time to think. I remembered the visit of my parents and brother, Dean, during the middle of my training. At that time, I had suddenly felt the full impact of the idea that people grow up, grow old, and die. Mother had been concerned about my dad's health. My brother, Dean, had already started getting into trouble. Unlike me, he was always caught. He couldn't lift a socket wrench from the five-and-dime without getting caught.

I remembered how relieved I'd felt when my family visited me, and I saw that Dad was looking real great and Dean was not on the FBI's most wanted list.

Now, recalling their visit, I asked myself, "Why?" Why did Dean and I seem to have this urge to do wrong? What was in us that kept getting us into trouble? Everything about my background cried out against this urge. If environment—and, for that matter, heredity—is responsible for man's conduct, then Dean and I had no excuse under the sun for the things we did.

Time after time, I "repented" of my behavior. Now restricted to the post, I vowed I would straighten up. The wild initiation party and my drunken AWOL escapades had already earned for me a reputation as a swinging drinker. These incidents merely brought out more openly what had been obvious to a few of my buddies all along—that I was really hooked on the bottle, and had been for months.

Time after time, I would renounce alcohol, vow to steer away from that arroyo of destruction my behavior was leading me to. And, time after time, I broke that resolution.

It never occurred to me to think about my relationship

with God, when worrying about my conduct and attitudes.

That didn't mean there were no experiences dangling before my eyes, trying to make me see a connection between problems I was having and a possible answer out of them. Now I know *God* was trying to tell me something—trying to get me to make this connection. Because there were two experiences during my military career that could have taught me a lot about the obvious relationship between my weaknesses and my neglecting to do any real thinking about God.

The closest I ever got to thinking about God was during the first two or three jumps at 1,000-foot altitude. On these occasions, I did condescend to "pray." "If there is a God," I said, "I would appreciate it if you will give me a safe landing."

One of the experiences I had that should have made me think more about God was my acquaintance with Marimatti. He was a devout Catholic who went to confession and Mass every Sunday morning. On weekdays and Saturday nights, he went out with Vern and me and the others, drinking, carousing and, in general, having a wild time. Yet, on Sundays, he'd go to confession, all pious—confess, be forgiven and know for dead certain that he was going to do the same thing over again during the week.

This kind of thing bothered me a lot, for years. Now I wonder why I was so bothered. At least, this guy was making an effort. What was I doing to get closer to God then? Nothing.

Instead, I sought the pleasures of the flesh. Vern and I ended up dating girl friends in a small town nearby. It was great fun for us. We'd pick up a case of beer and meet these girls at their apartment. They lived together and worked at the A&W Rootbeer stand as car hops. Saturday night we'd spend the evening doing whatever we wanted.

There was another fellow Vern and I knew, too, who gave us cause for some observations—from which I also failed to derive any lesson.

He was so religious that everyone called him *Preacher.* He always seemed to have great fun with a group of other religious fellows. I could not understand how he and his friends got so much pure joy from their Saturday night church meetings. It bugged Vern and me. So, we bugged him.

We invited him to come into the tent and sit down. Then we got our mouths in gear and really laid into him with *dare* talk. "If you're so spiritually strong, why can't you trust yourself to take a drink?"

At length he felt obligated to have a few social sips with us—which were enough to get to him. He was so unaccustomed to alcohol that after a half glass of whiskey in warm 7-Up, he was dizzy. He staggered out, talking in a kind of clip-tongued way. We followed him to see what he'd do.

For some reason, he went to the mess hall and into the kitchen. Near the door, he fell into a whole crate of eggs. Head first! He made an incredible mess—of himself as well as the kitchen floor.

Next time we saw Preacher, he was just as happy—with his group of guys—as though nothing had happened. It really galled me all over again that he could have so much fun doing "nothing" and that despite my bottles and broads, I never really, truly, had such joy as that which radiated from Preacher.

It especially puzzled me that he could have taken his shame so lightly, and could feel "clean" so quickly. After *my* escapades, I'd be in agony for days, feeling guilt cut me to the quick, reproaching myself for being such a drunken, lying slob.

After a cooling off period, I would do as the Catholic whom I condemned—go right back to the same thing.

At this point, it wasn't unusual for me to drink two-, three-, or even four-fifths of liquor during a weekend, and I was too dumb to see it was beginning to wreck me physically.

Because of my worship of the bottle, I nearly got killed one weekend. Vern and I and several other troopers went across the border into Tennessee, to one of our favorite joints where we knew some girls.

We had a blast that evening, drinking, dancing, kidding with the girls. As the night wore on, I became dimly aware of polarization taking place between the airborne group and the Tennessee farm boys.

There were about twenty of these backwoods guys to our five by the time the girls drifted off, and we were getting restless. After a couple of more drinks, the Fort Campbell group decided to leave and return to camp. Despite the insults that had been passed back and forth between the opposing group, our boys showed no awareness of danger. I got to my feet and started toward the door, ambling cockily.

As I started out the door, one of the Tennessee guys made an obscene gesture. I returned it, then turned my back on him.

From behind, I suddenly heard Vern shout. I whirled around. Two farm boys had him by the arms and were dragging him toward the back door. I took off after them and tackled one of them. There was a lot of commotion around us, including the loud juke box.

I suddenly found myself jumped by a couple more of the citizens, and the next thing I knew, I was staring at a switchblade held inches from my stomach. I was being backed out into the alley. I knocked the knife out of the boy's hand and grabbed him. We kind of danced around. I pushed him off and backed up to take a breath, but the drink I'd had ruined my timing. The next thing I knew I was hit by a haymaker that caught me right on the chin.

I hit the ground so hard large chunks of gravel gouged a long gash on my head.

Just before I passed out, I vaguely heard someone yell, "The cops are coming!"

When I woke up I was on the back seat of Vern's car. I felt the back of my head. My hand came away red and sticky with blood.

"We're taking you to an emergency hospital. One of the farm boys volunteered to tell us where it was," Vern said.

His companion in the front seat laughed. "Like, I volunteered for the draft."

"I'd say those farm boys don't cotton to dog faces," Vern said.

When the doctor saw me in another thirty minutes, he didn't laugh. He didn't seem to cotton to injured drunks, either. He stitched the gash in my head without giving me anything, and I had to interrupt the process to be sick. I threw up again on the way out.

Don Musgraves reported to his new duty station in Alaska wearing a huge bandage on the back of his head.

Our unit was sent up there to participate in a "practice" war to learn proficiency in Arctic weather and to defend the U.S. from Russia in case the Communists had any ideas of invading across the narrow Bering Straits.

We lived in small tents heated by tiny gasoline stoves and slept in special cold weather sleeping bags in several layers of clothes. At 25 to 50 degrees below zero, we were advised to stay off hard liquor because of the risk of having fingers and nose frost-bitten without our knowing it until too late.

I had a job typing transcripts for the provost marshal's department and driving. This was another occasion which, at this time, gave me some insight into criminals. Later, when I was on the other side of the law, I looked back on these experiences trying to figure out *why* I was always getting into trouble.

At the time, however, all I wanted was to get back to a place where I could practice my drinking without worrying about it causing me to lose a head or a foot, to get back to civilian life, actually. My discharge was coming up soon, and I couldn't wait.

A few months later, a free man, I got off the bus at Cushing, where my parents had moved a few months previously. I'd gotten a sense of my identity. I'd passed their hardest tests and won wings!

I strutted down the street to a taxi stand, then stood and looked around as civilians flowed around me. I stood there, waiting for a cab to show up, waiting for one of these civilians to *look* at me.

No one did. Everyone was wrapped in his own thoughts, bent on his own business.

Oh, well, I thought. My friends . . .

But soon I found all my friends were gone—or most of them: married, moved, vanished.

I was too arrogant and self-centered to be satisfied with my family's warm, loving reception.

Within a few days, I found that I was stirring up some interest after all.

The town seemed out to test returning servicemen, to find out what we were made of. During the first three or four months, I was involved in three or four fights I didn't start. It seemed to me they were staged deliberately. And no one was impressed with my new 1953 Oldsmobile.

But something else occurred which took my mind off the town's unfriendly attitudes. I walked into the corner drugstore to get a Coke and got hit right in the heart. The girl behind the counter was really something—beautiful, tall, with short-cropped flaming red hair and eyes like emeralds.

"I'm Don," I murmured as she put down my Coke.

"That's funny. I'm Donna."

"Donna? We'd make a good pair," I said, shaking the ice around in my glass. " 'Don and Donna' . . ."

I knew right then and there that I wanted to marry her. I didn't know a thing about her, but I was sure she was the right girl for me.

As she handed me the jar of drinking straws, I noticed she wore an engagement ring.

It was easy enough for me to get a date with her—which should have told me something right then and there. After a few dates on the sly, I held her close in the car one night and gently but firmly removed that other guy's engagement ring.

"Why don't you just give it back to him?" I asked. "I'll put one on. A better one. Bigger."

When this deal became public, the whole town had something else besides another cocky veteran to talk about: Don Musgraves had usurped someone else's place—shot somebody out of the saddle. I savored the prominence.

Naturally, the guy who lost didn't like the idea, but I guess he remembered how I'd scored in fights I'd been forced into. Instead of attacking me directly, he took it out on Donna. And my car. I'd lent it to her one afternoon so she could go shopping. She drove back in a few minutes. "The jerk tried to run me off the road!" she complained breathlessly.

I was furious. I don't know whether it was because

of what might have happened to Donna, or to that '53 Olds. I was really proud of her—the Olds. I made plans to take care of Herb.

I phoned a couple of people who knew Herb, pretending to be someone else wanting to know where I might find him that night. "It's urgent," I lied.

One of the guys said Herb would be parked out at a certain place in the boon docks with his new girl friend and another couple. I knew the place.

It was about 11 p.m. when Donna and I got there. I stopped behind his car and left my lights on. Blind with anger and shaking with rage I jumped out and went over to his car. He got out.

There were no preliminaries. I led with my right. I got two blows from him and then we went at it in earnest for about ten minutes. Donna cheered us both on while the people in his car just gawked.

We finally called it a draw. We were so evenly matched that, if we'd fought to the last, we'd have killed each other.

This fight established my reputation in the community as a tough guy. From that time on, no one else was willing to tackle me. Dean would have relished the reputation more than I, but I didn't do anything to disown it either.

Anything to give Don Musgraves an image!

I needed that image. Having the town kick me in the face a second time gave me a real inferiority complex. What was this anyway? A guy goes to school, wasting his precious youth learning to fit into society. He studies hard, goes by scout's rules pretty much—except for a few deviations, such as a little shoplifting, stealing, and drinking. Do all this and then graduate, get out, walk downtown, say, "Well, World, here I am. I'm ready. Show me all the goodies you promised." Then you get a boot in the face. You fall, and they kick you.

It was the same way with the Service. I suffered two years learning how to die. Taking insults from jokers who aren't fit to herd pigs, let alone shepherd human beings. "Sir" this guy and "Sergeant" that one, knowing he's nothing but a heel, a complete idiot who wouldn't be anywhere without his bars or stripes.

Then there was Betty. I go into all of this hell just

41

to make her proud of me. I suffer two years for my country and for Betty. Betty gives me the ax.

Anyway, when I finally serve my time, get out of this man's Army, what happens? The very punks I risked my life for, how do they express their gratitude?

They want to fight me.

How much of all this was my fault, and how much for real, that's up to a higher judge. I just know I was about to explode like a fragmentation grenade, or else shrivel up and die.

Until I met Donna. Until her saucy, laughing eyes winked at me, and her strange, crooked smile curled up.

It made me feel important to snatch Donna away from some creep who didn't deserve her, and to bring her under Musgraves' protective wing, the big guy, the tough guy, the good joe who always had a joke for everyone—or a fist.

Here was an image! I could laugh in their faces.

It was a whirlwind courtship. I didn't give her *time* to think. I had started college, really clawed right into it, brilliant from the word go.

As I stood in front of the preacher, ready to say "I do," I had every intention of being a good husband and having a good life with Donna. My optimism knew no bounds. She'd made me come alive again.

We rented a nice apartment and got in a few sticks of furniture. I promised Donna the moon in a few more months.

My image was complete! The great protector, provider, sage, and saint.

Oh, Lord, was I feeling great. High, *high* over the world.

"But Don," she said the day we were married. "Are you sure we should. . . ?"

"Listen, kid. I know this world better than you. I've been through it all while you were still going to the skating rink. I spent two years in Tennessee, Arkansas, Alaska. I've been to California. I know the ropes. Must listen to Daddy Don, baby—"

"But, I think—"

"I'll do the thinking. You just do the loving."

Every time she tried to suggest something, I already

42

had the answers. On the second day of our marriage, when she really went all out to try to finish a sentence, get a point across, express *her* feelings, I got a little upset.

On the fourth day, I got home late, real late. "I was out with the boys. Celebrating getting married, you know."

"No, I don't know. I—"

"You *don't* know? You'd better know it, honey. Now, come on, move over in that bed, baby. I'm crawling in—and don't fall asleep on me, either."

I came home from classes the fifth day after our marriage—after stopping for two or three drinks with a couple of classmates.

I came home hungry, anxious to see what kind of feast Donna had laid out for me *this* evening. I was only about thirty minutes late. She would have kept it warming. She'd light the candles when I walked in the door.

I was Mr. It and she'd have everything laid out on a silver platter.

Instead, there was a note on the silver platter: "Gone to Ma's."

She must mean that she had to go see her mother about something. Maybe the old gal was dying, or something. Maybe we were eating there tonight.

Still, I'd better look around.

Donna's clothes had disappeared from the closet. The overnight bag and suitcase were gone.

I rushed out of the house, jumped into the car, and tooled like crazy over to her parents' house. "She don't want to talk to you." Her old man glared at me. "And you'd best not push it."

So, what was the use? I had my answer. Musgraves had been taken. *Again!* A *second* time. Shafted. Used.

One of my friends said, "Don, you never gave her a chance. You overwhelmed her."

"You drink too much," another said. "Donna doesn't like booze."

Someone else said, "She just played you for a sucker. Boy, did you ever fall for it."

"Sucker?"

"He's right, Musgraves. Her real boyfriend wouldn't set a wedding date. She wanted to scare him into some action, man. It sure worked—for her."

I grabbed the guy by the shoulders and pushed him into the street. "Wipe that dirty smile off your stupid face," I spat.

I ran home crying.

Considering the circumstances, my parents let me move back in. They always had the door open for me. My dad, sick, bewildered, lied to get me an annulment, saying he hadn't given his permission for me to get married.

That part was easy. The rest of it was torture. For weeks, big, tough Musgraves lay in bed for hours, crying.

Now the town really had something to jaw about. Musgraves had got his "comeuppance." He swiped another guy's girl and she ditched him. Served him right.

The guys in the car pool I went to school with wouldn't let go of it. "Met any *girls* lately, Don? He, Haw. That was a joke, son."

"Who's cooking for you now, Musgraves?"

The whole town was jeering at me, driving me nuts.

I needed a drink . . . and another one . . . and one after that.

I managed to stick it out in school until the end of the spring semester by staying drunk, trying to study and getting my head on straight.

When school was out, I continued to blister under the town's scorn and, needing more money to buy booze, I looked around for a job. I didn't try very hard. My brain was whirling. I had to go—somewhere else, anywhere.

My grandmother on my mother's side had been visiting us and was returning to California. "I'll drive you there, Grandma," I offered.

"But, where'll you live, Don?" Dad asked.

"With me, of course," Grandmother said.

She was a real pal!

I took off under a cloud from that Oklahoma town, and I didn't plan to come back until I could swagger home, holding my head high, big enough to say, "I'm back, punks. You may now kneel."

44

Chapter 5

Grandma's house was still in a bit of country, and the orange groves left around her were a constant pleasure to her. I settled in, tried to put down my roots. She showered me with as much attention as she gave her plants, but I didn't respond like they did.

On the construction job I'd found, I earned over three dollars per hour carrying lumber, pouring concrete, digging ditches. I was strong and I had a lot of energy for both work and play.

I played hard that first summer, awed by the vast number of cocktail bars and night spots. Compared with Cushing and Stillwater, the local towns were dens of iniquity.

After the construction project played out, I looked around for something else. After a two-day wait at the union hall, I found another job on my own. I qualified as a machine operator somehow and started in right away on the swing shift at the Anaconda Wire and Cable Company. I was surprised to find that one of the guys there went full time to Santa Ana College during the day.

Well, I was working swing shift. I could do the same thing!

Realizing how much I wanted from life and comparing *that* with the rewards offered a machine operator, I hopped into my Olds and drove over to Santa Ana College where I was accepted and signed up for a full-time course.

At this moment, Don Musgraves was again the indefatigable dynamo for whom nothing, but nothing, was impossible.

And I proved it—for a while. The class work wasn't hard. I knew I had a good chance of getting a 4.0 grade average. By the end of the year, I'd been able to save a lot of money, in spite of my drinking, thanks to my full-time job, G.I. benefits, and Granny's modest demands for room and board.

Then the kind of thing happened that was beginning to become the story of my life. I met Ed Dunachek who liked to drink as well as I did. Ed was a motorcycle enthusiast. As had happened so often, I identified with my new friend—or we identified with each other.

I couldn't resist the temptation to buy myself a bike, too.

My role as dedicated scholar was forgotten. Musgraves was an easy rider now. The spring semester flew by like the telephone poles I raced past with wide-open throttle, my good intentions disappearing with the exhaust.

I started to play and drink so hard I could hardly make work or classes. The bike was the thing. I began to skip classes.

One night Ed and I took my car and stopped at a drive-in restaurant, looking for excitement. In the car next to us, Ed spotted Jan, a girl he knew. She introduced us to her friend, Loris Isaacs, sitting next to her.

Three days later, I was whizzing along on my bike when a girl waved to me from a car. I pulled over. It was Jan.

She whistled. "Some job, there." She was tall, skinny, with the sexy swing of a go-go dancer.

"The bike's got a lot of fire," I said.

She hopped on the back. "How about a joy ride?" This Jan didn't stand on preliminaries or ask for character references.

She hugged me around the waist as I took a corner on the sides of the tires. "Before I forget, my friend Loris is giving a party tonight. How about coming along?" She yelled in my ear.

That evening when I found Loris' house I was shocked to find that it was a *"girls only"* party and Jan wasn't there.

46

Loris came to the door and I explained that I didn't realize it was for girls only.

Something was different about Loris, something that made me prolong the conversation.

She was not like the other girls. She stood out like a lily among dandelions. I didn't think she'd go for any foolishness, so I was surprised that when I mentioned my bike, she asked, demurely, if she could take a ride on it some day.

It was the beginning of my friendship with Loris. I had her phone number and started calling her and just yakking. That spring, we began to date a lot, sometimes taking off on the bike to Irvine Park, twelve miles out of Tustin. You could stroll under the broad-branched trees, lie on the spacious lawns, and picnic, watch the ducks, or rent a boat and take your girl for a ride on the lily-padded water.

Loris and I dated but we also fought. We fought about my drinking, about my letting my studies take second or third place, and about our relationship getting too serious—or about my getting too ambitious some nights when it was warm and the moon was right.

I couldn't keep up the pretense of not being wild for her too long; when Ed and George and I got together, we didn't know when to stop drinking and roaring around on our bikes.

From one end of Orange County to another, we barrelled around, drinking, trying out new bars, trying out new girls, discussing life and its pleasures, and just wasting ourselves.

By the end of the spring semester, with only one month to go, I suddenly found myself completely burned out. I was the biggest mess I had been yet—completely empty, hurting, hollow. The worst was, *all my drive and ambition were gone.*

I woke up one morning, absolutely dying, and thought, "Where am I? *Who* am I?"

I couldn't even remember my own name for a few minutes. My own name!

Up until now, I'd been going to school full time and making straight A's, working full time and forgetting I needed sleep.

In a moment of trance-like unawareness and deep depression, I sold my bike for a song and informed the teachers I had to quit school. I gave no reason—just said there was an emergency.

Now, at this point there was just one thing to do: admit defeat, go back to Oklahoma, hang my head, and accept my punishment as a failure.

I hadn't done any of the big things in the Golden State which I'd started out so confidently, cockily, to do. My plans to come back to town swaggering, filthy rich, and lording it over the hicks had backfired in the smelly fumes of my bike's exhaust pipe.

I had noticed before there seemed to be a cycle to my life all right, and not a motorcycle. It was a cycle which now was repeating itself, that started with a surge, a burst of enthusiasm, blinding white light, energy, spiraling me into an orbit of ever increasing activity, an orbit in which I whirled faster and faster—until . . . the letdown!

Something—*someone*—*in* me was toying with my being. Someone who was *big*—big as the galaxy, the *universe!* —infinitely big. Big as creation . . . as *destruction.* Big enough to be the same sadistic force that played marbles with the stars. Someone as big as God. *Someone evil.*

I told Loris and her mother that I was through with school for the year.

I had to go home and see my parents and try to find myself again, to reestablish my identity.

As for all my savings, they'd been liquid. All drunk up. All I could think of was getting out on the road and driving, driving, driving, until I reached oil wells and Indians.

My folks were glad enough to see me. I'd come back to wallow in self-pity and to punish myself. Instead, I discovered how much I missed Loris! She had made a bigger impression on me than I wanted to admit.

I pondered our relationship almost constantly. She'd really gotten under my skin. I was even beginning to feel better already. But . . . I had nothing to offer her!

Why had I quit school?

Maybe . . .

I steeled my courage and talked to some friends who'd

gone to school with me that first year at Oklahoma State University. "Any ideas about some field to study for?" I asked one of them.

"Say, why don't you go and talk to my dean? He's in charge of the hotel and restaurant management training program."

The dean was encouraging. "Your credits can easily be transferred, young man," he said. "The field is wide open right now, Don. Knuckle down, hit the books hard, practice, and you can write your own ticket." Just like Dad.

I pondered it. Restaurant management sounded better than engineering. People have to eat. I liked dealing with people. I could see myself as the manager of a high-class restaurant, like some I'd seen in California.

With a career like that to look forward to, now I *had* something to offer Loris! Maybe she would marry me!

My future was falling into place—a new major, a new wife. Presto! Musgraves' magic!

I'd go back to California, win Loris as my bride, then take her back to Stillwater. I would enroll in the restaurant management program, work, study, keep my nose clean, and get my bachelor of science degree in restaurant management. We'd be on our way.

Up!

I was filled with fire again.

Abruptly, I said good-bye to my parents, and burned rubber all the way back to California.

My future was bright; there was no reason to doubt that Loris wouldn't go along with anything I suggested. After all, I was a pretty good catch, *now*, wasn't I? I had the looks and intelligence, two years of college with a good grade point and, now, a future.

I could see her face now as I proposed, dreamy and looking at me with those big hazel eyes. She had a special way of making me feel I was top dog.

I phoned Loris as soon as I got to Granny's house and sounded mysterious and overpowering and very, very anxious to see her the following night, when I'd be rested up and fit to make a good impression. "I've got some real surprises for you, honey," I promised.

The next day I drove into Los Angeles to see about

49

a job at Truman's, on Wilshire Boulevard. The Dean knew the manager and gave me a recommendation. I had to have some spending money if I was going to get married.

I landed a job at the restaurant! And that night, seeing Loris was as thrilling, marvelous, and joyous as I'd expected. She seemed to be caught up in my spirit, although she had no idea of the secret plans I had in store for her.

Truman's Restaurant was near the University of California, Los Angeles campus, although it was too high class and expensive for most of the students and professors. It had a drive-in department, coffee shop, separate dining room and facilities for large banquets.

"If you're going to take up this work seriously," the manager said, "there's nothing like starting as a short order fry cook. Don't sell it short, either, Mac. It's a real art, you'd better believe it."

It was true, man!

The next month was wild. After watching the other cooks, I discovered that I didn't know anything about anything, but I was quick and eager to learn. Very soon, I could whip out a good meal *in* short order with no beefs. The manager hadn't been kidding. Cooking quickly and skillfully was, man, like Picasso—art!

The bottles of wine for use in some sauces were always a big special help for *me*, too, I thought.

Loris saw that I was serious about my job and my new major. She was working for Virginia's Gift Shop at Knott's Berry Farm that summer, and we'd sit in the car during her lunch hour, or even ride the merry-go-round together. My "new look" really made her curious.

She saw that I had something on my heart.

One afternoon I asked her to meet me for lunch in the Chuck House, one of the Farm's eating places; then we went to my car to talk for a few minutes. I didn't wait for that moonlight night, but proposed right then and there, popping a ring I'd already picked out on her finger.

Having had all this in the back of my mind for some time, I was more prepared than Loris; she really flipped when I said, "Loris, marry me, will you?"

I held my breath like a mountain climber, feet dangling over a void. She nodded! Her hazel eyes shone.

I settled down to being a respectable young fiancé who was saving his scratch to get married and finish school.

All the trash and garbage had to be behind me. My new wife and I were going to make it. She'd depend on me, look to me for cues on relationships with other people. Her naive way was charming, but I knew it might cause trouble for her when we were away from friends, parents, protection.

At last I had found the key to happiness! Love at last had tamed Don Musgraves. Oh, I was so sure I had the complete answer to all my problems, troubles, pains, hurts, confusion!

Loris!

Of course, I knew that Loris and I were opposites in many ways. But I was so full of confidence—attraction of opposites, the perfect combination. We could teach each other.

The church that Loris and her mother chose for the ceremony was one in which she had worshipped enthusiastically all of her young life.

The night of August 31, 1957, I stood up at the altar of the Immanual Lutheran Church, a sea of faces staring at me, entrusting me with the beautiful hazel-eyed girl walking down the aisle on the arm of her father.

The Lutheran marriage service is beautiful and, as I stood close to my wife to be, I had all the best intentions of being a good husband that a twenty-two-year-old youth should have. I knew my worldly ways might frighten her sometimes, and I was prepared to be gentle with a girl who had had no experience with other men, had hardly been out of Orange County and had never traveled out of California.

I felt so protective!

We had a four-day trip to Oklahoma for a honeymoon, in a car packed so full of things, there was only room for us to sit behind the steering wheel together.

It was another eighty-mile-an-hour trip, except that we stopped for one night and day in Riverside, south of Los Angeles. Our honeymoon night was a brand-new experience for Loris and, in a sense, for me. It revealed ourselves to each other in a way neither had known before. It was a beautiful, mysterious night.

When we arrived home, the car loaded down with wedding gifts, my parents were overjoyed. The gifts and our recounting of the wedding made Mom feel as if she'd been there herself. "Loris, you must be exhausted," she said, hugging her. Mom didn't notice that Loris hung back.

Dad sat in a corner of the living room and shook his head. "Don, I don't see how you do it." He winked at me. "No wonder you were so hot to go back to California to get her."

I was in Seventh Heaven! I had returned home in triumph, after all, to give the horse laugh to those snotty small town hicks who'd sneered at me before. I'd come home with a girl more beautiful, faithful, and charming than Donna could ever be. And I'd made plans to embark on a dignified, profitable college course leading to status, means, and security in a business that was really where it was at. Wherever that was.

It didn't dawn on me that Loris was feeling out of it, with me getting the lion's share of attention from my family; or that she was already homesick, missing her own parents; or that my parents, so warmly possessive, overwhelmed her.

Chapter 6

It was a good thing Loris and I moved into a place owned by nice landlords. Mr. and Mrs. Carmichael were in their late seventies and they treated us like a son and daughter.

Loris became very friendly with the Carmichaels. It didn't occur to me that she had no one to talk to while I was in school and working full time so soon after our short honeymoon.

Oklahoma must have seemed a very strange place, after living in Southern California all her life. Oklahomans' way of being friendly might seem overbearing and nosey at times, and Loris didn't know how to respond.

She didn't warm up to campus life as Mrs. Don Musgraves either. At home, and before I married her, she was always gay and smiling and, even though she was quieter than I, her personality always won people over. Now when I introduced her to my friends, she was just the opposite.

When we went places I was always so proud of her, but I guess I forgot to tell her. I forgot to tell her a lot—how much I loved her, how much I needed her constant reminders that I was Mr. "It" in her life. I didn't realize she needed reassurance, too—reassurance that what I was doing away so much was for both of us.

She often cried her eyes out at night when I didn't get home until very late, for as soon as I finished classes, I worked as a full-time cook in the coffee shop at the Student Union Building. This was part of the curriculum. Then we would head for the nearest study hall—one of the guys' homes. We would study our way through a fifth of scotch and be bombed by ten or eleven o'clock, then stagger home. That wasn't a required part of the curriculum.

Working my way up from salad maker, waiter, and fry cook to assistant manager, I was gone more and more. Loris decided crying wasn't going to help, so she found a job as a checker at a dry cleaner's and joined the forces of working wives helping put their husbands through college.

My mother didn't make things any better, either. She wanted to love and accept Loris like a daughter, but when we were together, Loris thought she was paying more attention to me than necessary and she was jealous. Whenever I'd ask Mom's advice or opinion or anything, Loris would take it as a personal insult, assuming I didn't think *her* advice valid.

In order to pacify Loris, I started seeing less of my parents. It was a strain anyway, since we were so busy. We became acquainted with another couple instead of Jim and his wife, Mary, but Loris couldn't warm up to them, either.

One night after Jim and I had been studying particularly late, he started home. We had killed at least two bottles of whiskey, and Jim didn't function too well. I should have stopped him, but I couldn't even *see* straight. He got into his car and tore off down the street. Loris had just started getting ready for bed when we heard a chilling screech followed by a jarring crash. It seemed to come from just around the corner.

It was Jim. He had run a stop sign and hit another car. Fortunately, he hadn't had time to get up much speed, and, having had so much to drink, he didn't even know if he was hurt.

"I saw it all," an elderly lady cried. "This young fellow didn't even stop. Why, he's been drinking, too. Look at him! He can't even stand up."

"It serves him right." Someone else spoke up. "He shouldn't even be allowed a license."

Loris tightened her grip on my arm. "Don, that could have been you!"

54

"Hah!" I laughed. "I know better than to drive when I'm feeling that way."

Loris accepted that, then, but I don't remember how many times I never knew what "that way" was.

Alcohol was more and more important to me. It was the "tide over" between classes, work, studying, and more classes—working and studying.

I didn't stop to think of what alcohol might be doing to my mind and body. I was even beginning to develop a potbelly from so much boozing, late hours, and poor eating habits.

Both my heart and body ached for Loris, but I couldn't help her because I couldn't help myself. She was beginning to look more tired each day.

As assistant manager, I was beginning to *feel* my job. I knew I had chosen the right profession. I could see the golden future. "This is it," I thought. "This is the way I want things to click after I graduate." Here I was, already working in a beautiful $10,000,000 building that was grossing two million dollars per year. I was being looked up to by waitresses, students, and the bosses who were beginning to watch me very closely.

At the beginning of my second year at the university, I was acquiring skills at a rapid pace. The profit I could show my boss at the end of the month sent my self-confidence sky-high. Hardly anyone who came into the coffee shop was a stranger to me. Hardly a person I passed on the campus didn't call out a hello.

I was the eye of an Oklahoma tornado whirling with irresistible force cutting a pathway along the landscape for *Mr.* Musgraves!

One night after a big rush at the coffee shop and some big news from the boss, I went home full of self-importance to find Loris, with candles on the table and a bright tablecloth.

"Don," she said, "I've seen you only one night this week." The words fell heavily over a warmed-over dinner. "I know you're getting busier at the coffee shop, with your new job, but there's something I want to tell you."

"Well, there's something I want to tell you, too, honey." I'd been hugging the news to myself all day and I couldn't wait to explode with it.

"Go ahead, then," she suggested, reaching over and putting her hand on mine.

She looked pretty in the candlelight, I thought. She had her own special glow tonight. Maybe... "Look, honey: we'll have to take in a movie this weekend, or something to celebrate. I can't keep it from you any longer." I took a deep breath and blurted out the news, "I've been promoted to *manager* of the whole coffee shop—something that's never been allowed in the entire student program. The boss just told me today." I grinned. "He wants... well, it'll mean I'll have to spend more time in meetings. Oh, like tonight... I have to go back. But honey, just think: the *manager!* And I haven't even graduated yet. What do you think of that?"

I squeezed Loris' hand. No response. She just sat and stared at me. "That's great, Don... but... oh, *no*— it's *not* great." She jerked her hand out of mine and ran from the room, knocking over her chair.

The door slammed, shaking the wall. "Loris!" I yelled. "What's gotten into you?" I went into the bedroom. She was standing with her back to me, facing a corner.

"You wouldn't understand if I told you," she sobbed. "Besides, you might be late for your *meeting* with your boss, and I wouldn't want them to blame me." Her words were a slap across the face—the way she said them.

"Look, honey," I said, trying to be patient. "I'm not going until you tell me what's going on. Look, sweetheart, whatever it is, we can talk about it. I wouldn't be able to do all these things if it weren't for you. Don't you know that?" I hadn't really looked at or listened to Loris for many months. Now she was demanding my attention.

"I went to the doctor last week," she began haltingly. "I've been getting sick in the mornings for the past month, missing about an hour of work each day, having to come home and lie down."

"What did the doctor say?" I asked, standing up excitedly. "What'd he say? Why didn't you tell me right away?" I was ready to sink through the floor at the thought something might be wrong with Loris. Suddenly I felt something of that love buried beneath all the debris of work, study, and drink.

"Look, honey," I continued. "It can't be too bad. With all the modern medical miracles nowadays, the doctor will have you fixed up in no time."

Suddenly, she began to chuckle, then burst out laughing. "Oh, darling. I'm sorry." She was still laughing. "I didn't mean to mislead you. We're going to have a baby. That's why—"

"A baby. You're kidding. A kid? Now, wait a minute. You mean, you're pregnant? I mean, before I graduate and get a job? Before we really. . . ?"

A sudden picture went through my mind of my grandmother telling me about when I was born in the cotton fields. There weren't any facilities and Mom had had to wash diapers by hand. I didn't want Loris to have to do this. If I'd even given any consideration to having a child, it would have been after we'd had a house with a big yard, at least two cars, and a nursery.

I started to explain what I'd had in mind about the timing—but decided to cool it. "Well, baby, that's real neat. I kept wondering why you've been looking so beautiful lately." I shook my head. "You're a tricky one!" I glanced at my watch.

Now I had to leave or be late for a very important meeting. "Uh, it's too much to ask you to stay up for me, but would you mind if I woke you up when I come back from the meeting? You might want to hear about it."

She didn't answer immediately. Then—"No. I'll try and rest while you're gone." She smiled.

I literally flew over to the Student Union Building to meet with the bosses. Before they could say anything, I told them about the baby. I figured it would impress them about how serious I was—establish the young family-man image.

Well, I'd just have to work that much harder. With the restaurant business, it looked as though you could get to the top pretty easily if you just used your head and kept on the good side of the right people. My mind finally jerked back to the meeting.

We went into the inner office and the boss told me what he expected of a manager, what kind of reports he wanted, what types of employees he wanted hired. As assistant manager, I was already familiar with a lot of this but it helped to go over it, identify myself with being told what to do.

Loris looked rested when I returned and we had a conversation, a real conversation about things that mattered to us. We talked about the business, our future, our baby. It was good just to be with her and hold her again, and I made a vow to myself that I'd try to make it home sooner at night. After all, I was going to be a father. A father needs love and understanding, too.

"Move over, baby, and I'll rock you to sleep."

The pressures on me were now enormous. As a full-time manager of a large food service organization and a full-time student learning how to be the *ideal* manager, I was in a constant whirlwind of activity. The prospect of becoming a father was just one more of the pressures, and I had developed the habit of responding to pressure by hitting the bottle. Now I hit it harder than ever.

As though there were need for any additional encouragement to drink, the flattery of my many new friends supplied more. I always felt I had to repay attentions with a round of drinks, or accept drinks in the spirit of camaradarie.

Michael Musgraves was born on September 1, 1959. Loris was busy, busy enough not to notice that now *I* was getting sick. The alcohol in my bloodstream was saturating every cell! The aspirins I swallowed daily didn't help the headaches anymore. By the time I got to the coffee shop, I'd take a swig of whiskey "to calm my nerves," and to try to stop the aching. Then if I didn't eat right, my stomach would act up and it was easy to take another drink—and another.

This went on for the better part of my senior year.

Somehow, I was doing a great job in my classes and the fact that I was holding down a manager's job lent prestige to my role as a student, especially in personnel administration. The professor used me as an example!

"Now, Don," he'd say, "when you have a personnel problem—for instance someone continually asking for time off and you know they don't deserve it or you can't afford to give it to them, what do you do?"

I always had the answers.

One day, Mom came over to see us. I'd been on a field trip and when I got back, I was really messed up. I'd had a headache when I left in the morning, but by the time I returned, the pressure in my head was so great I was irrational. Pain seemed to be picking at my brains.

Loris wanted to take me to the hospital, but the baby was just waking up for a feeding. Mom said she would take me to her doctor.

Mom's doctor was a chiropractor. "Sounds like you've got sinus trouble, boy," he said while he laid me out on the table. He put a scope on my spine to measure the nervous tension in my muscles. I didn't know what that had to do with my head.

He scratched his head. "Boy, I can't figger how you're still walking around. Your nerves are so out of whack, you should be curled up and crippled like a possum after a hound hunt.

"Y'all realize that your nerve endings are calcified?" he asked as he painfully manipulated my toes. "Jest plum solidified! I got to break this loose, so hold on and don't buck too much."

I moaned and wished someone would give me a drink. When he was finished with me, I couldn't even bend my toes.

At home, I lay in bed drowning in self-pity. I was too close to reaching my goals, too close to finishing school. Everything counted on my getting that little piece of white paper in my hand. Everything was riding on me. If I didn't get that degree, I wouldn't make it in the business world. We wouldn't have the things we wanted. Why were they doing this to me now?

I was forced to lie flat in bed the next day. But the morning after that, I got up. I was able to blow my nose and I began to feel some relief. In fact, I felt almost human. Loris and I were able to talk about some of my problems, mainly drinking. We both decided that, as soon as I graduated and picked the spot I wanted to work in, had two cars in the garage, the house we wanted, wall-to-wall carpeting, all the latest time-saving devices for Loris—all the symbols of the good life, and all that—*then* I'd stop being a creep and drinking so much.

"It's just all this tension and insecurity," I said, "that's making me like this."

With that in mind, the following week, after returning to school and the coffee shop, I accepted a job offered by Mannings. Loris and I both decided that California was where we wanted to live and the Los Angeles area held the most promise. Loris' folks still lived in Orange, which I'm sure had a bearing on *her* eagerness.

Graduation was a big moment in our lives, but it was soon followed by chaotic packing and good-byes to my family and all our friends and the employees I had worked with. My professors thought I had made a good choice. Manning's Cafeterias was a highly reputable chain of about 100 eating establishments in the West.

I thought I had made an excellent choice because I was getting a raise of $75 over my present salary.

Everything we owned was packed into a trailer this time. We were jubilant about going back to California. While driving, we talked about where we would like to live and what we were going to do with all the money I was going to make. There was no doubt in our minds that I would do well. I had already proved myself at the University, hadn't I?

In Los Angeles, after looking all day, we found a dumpy apartment in a rundown neighborhood, but the rent was right and it had all the utilities and basic needs plus two bedrooms. Coming home each night to the area depressed me. I kept thinking about all those fancy places we'd seen, the well-lit streets and locked play areas. Here, I had to park my car out by the back alley, lock it, and hope for the best.

The first day I went to work at my new job, they had forgotten I was going to come. The manager wasn't there. The assistant to the assistant manager was a nice, milk-toast guy who didn't seem to have any words of his own. "I'll have your job soon," I thought to myself as he showed me around.

The layout itself impressed me. They'd spent wads of money. "Well, where do I start?" I asked.

"Why, uh, the kitchen, of course," he muttered. "You'll

want to understand what goes on in every job in this place. From the ground up. In order to do it the *Manning's way*, you'll do each job until you have completely mastered it. Periodic evaluation will determine whether you're ready for the next step.

"Of course, it goes without saying—any suggestions you come up with for ways on cutting down inefficiency on the job will be welcome."

My spirits rose a little. "Do you need any help in figuring food costs? That was one of my specialties at the university. Even the professors couldn't figure out how I could cut down on their estimated food-cost sheets. I ended up saving the management—"

"Excuse me, Don," he interrupted. "I'll talk with you more some time. Right now, I've got to get back to work." He gestured toward gleaming, stainless-steel sinks and to the chef on duty. "Steve will show you what needs to be done here before the next rush. He'll be your trainee manager for the next few months while you're in the kitchen."

Steve explained the layout of the kitchen and my duties. It all sounded so familiar, I started drumming my fingers on the counter and turned him off—that is, until he pointed to the pile of pots and pans in the far corner. "No Man's Land" was one of the names for that corner. It was always hot, steamy, and crowded, and you had to watch your step on slippery boards supposed to keep your feet dry.

"That'll be your baliwick for a while," he said. "Make sure you keep up with me, once the rush starts. None of the chefs like it when they reach for a favorite pot and it isn't there."

The kitchen had been fairly empty when we first started talking, but now it was a bustle of noise and commotion, each person busy at his station. One by one, they gave me a nod.

"Hey, you're one of the new 'trainees,' ain't you?" someone shouted. A wild, sadistic giggling spread around the kitchen. "How long are you in for?" someone else asked.

A black guy washing dishes—or, rather, loading a dishwasher that spewed out scalding steam—bent close. "I started out on this trainee's program two years ago."

But I wasn't going to let them get me down. I dove

into that corner, removed my jacket and tie, rolled up my sleeves, and started the old pot-washing routine. I knew it well—scrape, rinse, soak, scrub, rinse, and lay on the rack. Over and over and over and over. One by one, they would disappear as the busy boys put them away. One by one and sometimes two by two, they would *re*appear. By the end of the shift, my eyes were watery, my back ached, and my hands looked much worse than those television ads for lotion.

I lost track of time in that corner. I couldn't even come up with a new way to wash a pan.

One day I remembered that chefs have a supply of wine. On the sly I helped myself to some of the choice brandies. That got me through the next four hours. At my half-hour break, I made a break across the street and had a couple more drinks.

By the time my shift ended, I was well on my way to feeling better. But it wore off. With still a bit of a glow on, however, I decided I would take a bottle of wine home to Loris. We'd celebrate.

Coming home to a small apartment with a wife on a strict grocery budget isn't the best of homecomings.

"Don," Loris cried. "You're early and I haven't even started dinner. I was going to run down to the store and . . . " She trailed off when she saw the bottle of wine I put on the table.

I poured the wine and raised my glass to her. "Let's celebrate. Let's celebrate the fact that I just spent four years in college, graduated with a three-point average with a B.A. in management and a minor in hotel and restaurant management. *Then*, I was chosen by Manning's, Inc.—"

"Don—"

"Did they want me to start out as an assistant manager? No . . . 'You'll need to be trained the *Manning's way*, Don. *Perhaps* in a few months. . . .' Well, did they put me on as the purchasing manager? I really whaled in that subject in school. No. Well, maybe at least the assistant to the assissssttttttant manager. Then after a decent interval, like maybe three months, we would move into a classy apartment, one with some elbow room, maybe even a wading pool. Where you could at least have friends in. Or, maybe, they'd at least recognize me at the restaurant as someone who *knows* something, not just one of the paid help!"

I stood up, staggering a bit, then gestured toward the kitchen. "I worked my way up from *pot washing* to manager of a two-million-dollar corporation. *Now,* what am I doing? *Learning how to wash pots, the MANNING'S WAY."*

I poured myself the last of the wine, gulped it down, then put my head down on the table and cried.

Chapter 7

The curvy slave girl in the see-through robe of finest embroidered silk crept shyly and fearfully into the throne room, made the necessary obeisances with her slim, graceful hands, saying, "Salami!" as she did so, and approached closer to me as I lounged, sipping an exotic Oriental drink, in a cushioned chair with carved arm rests. At my careless gesture, she prostrated herself on the carpeted floor and kissed my manicured toes peeping out of my bejeweled slippers. When she looked up, her seductive brown eyes were eager. "You rang, your Lordship?"

"Yes, I wish you to enscribe an epistle to the Oasis Date Corporation, Inc. Oh, uh, just tell them we want a dozen cartons of their finest grade. And, as for you, I wish to schedule a personal date tonight."

Well, it might as well have been like this. Don Musgraves had really hit it big. I was now the assistant manager of an $80,000-a-month "link" in the Manning's chain, a "store," as we called it in the trade, which employed one hundred people and enticed hundreds of customers daily off the streets—Wilshire Boulevard, in Los Angeles, to be exact—along the Miracle Mile.

I had my own plush office with thick red carpeting, a gigantic polished imitation mahogany desk, a sleek filing cabinet, a bookcase full of impressive looking volumes on management, mass feeding, and culinary magic.

My blonde private secretary *did* wear lovely, soft, clinging blouses and tight skirts, and I had an assistant, a real cool guy who, like me, subscribed wholeheartedly to all the good things in life, including good times.

I could call on the telephone just about anywhere in the world without worrying about toll charges. My secretary screened my phone calls. I wasn't to be bothered by cranks and others who might interfere with my swinging sub-executive life. I had merely to mutter and it would be obeyed by any of several dozens over whom I had particular authority.

I could have the finest steaks smothered with the tenderest mushrooms and exotic sauces any time of the day or night I chose, even have them delivered to my private office if it were my whim.

I was really living!

In that short year since Loris and I had had our momentous discussion about what it would take to get Musgraves' head back on straight, I had fulfilled just about all the specifications far above and beyond what we had anticipated.

Oh, I worked for it—fourteen hours a day, seven days a week some weeks. I opened the place in the early morning and closed it down at night, and I didn't spend all that much time in my plush private office. As the assistant manager, I was on the go most of the time. There were frequent conferences with employees, including our skillful chefs, many leisurely chats on and off duty with our psuedo-sophisticated bartenders, and lots of friendly conversations with our shapely waitresses.

My boss expected results, but he didn't restrict me or investigate how I used my time—and I had to make good use of it to keep things running smoothly. Mine was a position of big responsibility.

I really had it made—except for one thing: I wasn't making enough money. I had received several raises along with promotions during the few months it had taken me to rise to this pinnacle. But I wasn't making enough to support Loris, Michael, myself—and Tom Collins.

Right now I was making nearly $600 per month. It wasn't a big deal, but it could have been enough to live on. And, after all, I was just starting out. The future looked great. It was a good enough start for any guy, except when you are providing room and board for Mr. Collins. And—I hate to say it—I also was sharing my liquor with a bevy of girls.

I was alone in my throne room—er, office—one afternoon, having instructed my secretary, Roxie, not to disturb me. I wanted an hour by myself just to think.

I thought I was alone. But suddenly, I heard a voice. "Don Musgraves. . . ." It was an eerie, hollow voice. I looked around, my heart racing.

Forget it! I picked up some papers and quickly sifted through orders, invoices, memos, while my mind raced over the months since Loris and I had arrived in California.

Our lowest ebb was when I broke out crying while we were sharing that bottle of cheap wine. In just a few weeks after that, things began to look up. They tried me out on some other jobs besides pot-washing. Soon, I was riding around with the assistant to the assistant manager, helping him buy produce.

I related what I observed to my earlier experiences when I would listen to my dad deal with wheels. Mentally, I practiced my own approach. After a while, I was suggesting things to Bill, the assistant. Presently, Bill was sitting back, letting me do the talking. "I'm leaving for 'Frisco soon," he confided one day. "A big job. Take that for what it's worth."

I could see what was on the horizon. I was being groomed to take Bill's place.

If I idolized Bill for his sharp managerial qualities, I worshipped the manager and assistant manager, Bob and Ralph. They were my gods. *They* really had it made. They were successful, important men of the world.

For a short while, this illusion lasted. I suddenly found myself made assistant to the assistant manager. In the weeks that followed, I tagged these guys around like a puppy dog. I imitated them slavishly. They knew where it was at.

Then the bubbles started bursting.

"Don," Bob burst out when we were in his lavish office one morning. "I've really had some shafts thrown at me lately. I'll bet you think Ralph and I are—like that." He twined two fingers together. Ralph was the assistant manager. "In public, we have to maintain an image."

I grunted. "I don't follow you."

"He's always played it so cool. We got to be real friendly. Know what I mean? Real buddies. The fact that I was the manager and he was my assistant— you know, we don't go for a lot of stiff-necked stuff around here. Anyway, I invited him and his wife over for dinner one night. The next thing I knew, he was inviting my wife and me over. It got to be a regular thing—two, three, four times a month we'd get together for this or that. Getting drunk together, sometimes, too. Dancing. The bit. Anyway, you know what I found out after several months?"

Was this a guessing game?

"He was meeting my wife on the sly. Naturally, we fix our work hours so when I'm on, he's off. And visa versa. So, he takes advantage of it. They were really making it. The whole way, know what I mean? So, you know what happened yesterday? I filed for divorce, that's what happened."

I gulped. "I'm sorry to hear that."

The manager bent forward. "I feel like killing him."

"You could fire him."

"Then it would all come out. As it is, it's just a quiet court case, a tiny item—maybe—buried in the paper, if it's even reported."

This hit me hard. I had built up all this idealism about guys in their positions, their holiness, good character, superiority in everything. These were the guys I was desperately, ambitiously trying to emulate.

Then I find out they get involved in the same sordid scrapes as the rest of us peasants.

Why did it bother me so? This, I cannot explain. Maybe I was trying to resist this kind of thing in my own nature. Could it be that my exaggerated reaction to their petty troubles was really a rationalization for my own future conduct? I'd wanted to do this all along, but had to find an *alibi*? In high school I'd succumbed to the temptation to steal. In the Army, I'd become famous for the quantity of liquor I could consume. At Oklahoma

State University, I'd been drunk almost constantly—had physical breakdowns because of it. I'd even cheated on Loris!

Maybe I wanted to go back to that kind of life, and I could, pertending I'd been terribly, terribly let down at seeing my idols crumble.

At the time, however, I didn't try to analyze it. I just let my emotional reaction have its head. I started drinking more heavily. Staying out later, later, later.

I'd passed up a lot of chances with the pretty waitresses whom I helped hire, but I was in a position to make the most of the opportunity when, a few weeks after my talk with Bob, the assistant manager *was* fired and I was appointed to replace Ralph. Now, as assistant manager, I had the waitresses crawling at my feet. I could pass out the favors—or withhold them. I could extract my pound of flesh. And I started to do just that!

I began to drink even more, stay out even later, ignore Loris and Mike. I lied to cover my absences from home. One time I told Loris the police had detained me overnight. She didn't really buy that one, but there was no way she could check up. Rather, her efforts to do so—I learned much later—were futile. The police wouldn't tell her yes or no. In this case, they were on my side—for a change!

I was becoming a great story teller! One time, in the wee hours of the morning, I had to go through the bedroom to get to the bathroom; I crept as silently as I could, because I was covered with mud. If only I could have gotten to the bathroom and gotten cleaned up before . . . But, no! Loris was awake, as usual.

"Don!" she said from the bed. "Your best sport coat! You're covered with mud. That'll have to go to the cleaners again. What happened?"

"Oh, uh, it's this way, Loris," I stammered, standing unsteadily in the middle of the bedroom, trying to keep out of the glow of the night lamp. "This guy came at me. . . ."

I was sure I had Loris conned. The truth of the matter was, I had gotten so drunk I'd fallen in a ditch.

Loris was pregnant with Lynne then and trying to take

care of Michael, still a toddler. Much later, she said, "I felt so helpless, so hopeless. There was nothing I could do to help you."

She cried her heart out many nights. All she could do was pray for me, ask God at least to bring me home safely. Night after night after night, after a long day keeping house, she suffered tortures.

I did nothing in return for her efforts. Nothing but drink more and more and more.

As I idly sifted through the bills, employee rating sheets, daily cash receipt reports, thinking back on all these things, trying to convince myself that the pressure wasn't getting to me, worrying about money, wondering how I'd pay for all the drinking, I heard that voice again! Eerie, hollow, echoing: "Don Musgraves."

This time it went on: "You agree, they're not paying you what you're worth. You say, 'Some day they will.' Don't you? How about the big boss? How about Bob? Now there's a guy that has it made. You think so, eh?" There was a profound silence. "Uh, uh. They'll never pay you what you're worth. Why don't you just take a peek at his check some time? Just hold it up to the light?"

A week or two later, when the checks came to my desk for distribution, I couldn't resist the temptation to do what the Voice had suggested—and I did and it was right.

Even the big boss, Bob, wasn't making what I thought *I* was worth!

"I told you so," the Voice echoed suddenly. "You're going to have to make up the difference."

Voice, demon, or my subconscious—whoever it was, I had to agree with it.

I started ripping off money.

Four times a day we collected the money from the cash registers, put it in envelopes in a safe that could not be opened until the armored car pickup came.

I stuffed the money into the envelopes all right. But, as I dropped the unsealed envelopes in the safe, my fingers slipped in to grab one or two bills, sometimes a one or five-dollar bill, sometimes a ten or twenty.

Not to get anyone too excited, I kept my pilfering

the losses. They suspected the cashiers. It didn't occur to me I was causing grief to a lot of people, enmeshing many others in a net of suspicion.

A close eye was kept on the cashiers and waitresses, but the amount of the losses was too small to warrant a full-scale investigation.

I would probably have gotten away with it for a long time, except that one night someone got in the bottom safe and ripped off several thousands of dollars. This did it.

Now, they suspected the managers, the assistants. All of us were "asked" to take lie detector tests. While I was able to answer the specific questions about the looting of the safe quite satisfactorily, the reading showed a variation. The Los Angeles Police Department technician who administered the tests retested me once, twice, three times. Then he shook his head.

"I've got to come up with a logical reading," he told me when we were alone. "You're hiding something, aren't you, Musgraves?" He talked some more, then said, "Listen, the main thing is satisfying myself as to the cause of the deviation. For my report, I'll make a deal. Level with me and, if it doesn't have anything to do with the safe job, we'll just forget it. Okay?"

I shrugged. I was tired. I needed a drink. "Okay." I told him the story.

He shook his head. "Sorry to hear that. Listen, Musgraves. If I cover for you, will you try to be a good boy and keep your fingers out of trouble?"

When I returned to work, something was in the air —in Bob and Jim's tone of voice. Still, no one said anything directly. Of course, I decided to cool it for a while, just to make sure.

After a couple of weeks I was crawling the walls, the alcoholic content of my blood reduced to too low a level because of lack of funds; and I decided to risk it again.

In a short time, I was the old familiar, slap-happy, smiling Don Musgraves—by day; and a sodden, stinking Mr. Hyde by night, haunting noisy, smoky dives, getting sick in parking lots in the dark early hours of the morning, staggering along the sidewalks of hell . . .

Then Bob asked me to relieve managers in other

stores which hadn't reported any losses. I thought they were preparing me for a supervisory position with the main office!

When losses began to occur in these other stores, too, on the days when I was acting manager, Bob had the goods on me.

I was called into the main office where I signed a sworn statement.

"Of course, that means you're fired," Bob said after I'd handed back the statement in which I'd left blank the total amount involved. (How should I know how many hundreds of dollars I'd lifted from those cash registers? I didn't have an accountant to go over my books.) They both avoided my eyes.

"Yeah, it figures." I walked out of that office with every intention of committing suicide. I couldn't face being exposed as a thief, fired and jobless. There was no explanation I could give Loris that would even satisfy *me*.

It was two o'clock in the afternoon when I walked out. I drove around until ten at night. I don't remember much of the long, joyless ride on Los Angeles' pretzel freeways.

Driving, I tried to decide how I would kill myself. Run my car off the freeway? Jump off that famous bridge in Pasadena? I finally ended up sixty miles away, in San Bernardino, unable to get up enough nerve to eliminate myself from the environment I was polluting.

I finally went home. It took another two hours to tell Loris what had happened. We were both tired. She'd been up with Michael, had been sick as her term with Lynne neared, and she had worried half the night wondering where I was.

Now she had to sit up with me several hours, knowing by my drunken epithets something really traumatic had happened. Bleary-eyed, we both became emotional. And then I let her have it—straight between the eyes: "I got caught stealing money and got canned."

I thought for a while I'd have to call the men in white. It was the worst I'd seen her. The news really shook her.

When we finally cooled down a little, it was daybreak

and we'd decided the best thing to do was to confess all to the pastor of the Lutheran church where Loris still faithfully went.

Actually weeping, I told the pastor about stealing money and my involvement with other women.

The minister said nothing about the love and forgiveness of the Lord. Instead, he advised me to go through the sixteen weeks of "instructions in the faith" and, at the end of that period, seek baptism. He also advised us to confess all these things to *Loris'* parents! I saw no reason to confess to my in-laws, but I figured he must know best. All it accomplished was to expose myself as a thief and a drunk, a terrible man whom they had suspected for years.

I started singing in the choir, but before I could utter a note I had to drink a bottle of wine. I took the sixteen weeks of instructions, then was asked if I wanted to be baptized. It was a water baptism, and as soon as the pastor sprinkled me with water, I realized that neither the water nor the sixteen weeks had done a thing to change Don Musgraves. I felt the same way I had before. The pastor hadn't stirred me about Jesus. It was in one ear and out the other.

I didn't want to expose myself again to the temptations of the restaurant business, but this was the only job I was qualified for. Lying about my past, I got a job in a recently opened restaurant which was operating in the red. In the first month, I cut the loss in half; then this thing that possessed me, that seemed to live in my fingers, came to life again and the next thing I knew, I was dipping into the till as well as swiping liquor from the bar.

Of course, I was fired.

After a week of feeling sorry for myself, I went out job hunting again. Nationwide Food Service needed an assistant manager for its inplant food contract with North American Aviation plants. I went to Autonetics in Anaheim, and in filling out my application I did away with a whole year of my life, leaving out my experience at Mannings. Despite the fact that North American gives applicants a tough check, including police records, they didn't bother to check with Oklahoma State University as to when I'd graduated. I was in.

The NFS concessions in the various aircraft plants

was operated through a self-service, reach-in deal, like a New York City automat. Customers reached into the pigeon holes for food in plastic containers and paid the cashier at the end of the line.

I was trained to manage three different plants, then promoted to manager of all three. At work, things went well. I felt emotionally secure *while on the job*. I was getting a livable wage, but it turned into the same old story: it wasn't enough to support all the drinking I was doing after work.

Drunk every night, I was staying out later and later. Often I'd only get home in time to change clothes and go back to work.

And I was becoming violent. I'd tear up the house. I was fighting—something! Something inside, though I didn't know it then.

I took it out on my dear, patient, suffering Loris! I threw her against the wall a couple of times like throwing a rag doll. Jack the Ripper was inside of me. Strange I didn't end up killing someone.

I had the shakes all the time and was sick at work. My hand shook so much I could hardly dial a telephone.

I returned about four o'clock one morning, strung out. The night seemed to have devoured me, gulping me down into a maw of surging acid before spitting me out. I crept into the bedroom. Loris was groaning in her sleep. One part of me wanted to reach out and touch her, awaken her with soft words. But who was I to do that? I was a total catastrophe, my clothes wrinkled and dirty, my body smelly and cold, my face feeling like it must have a thousand wrinkles of pain and nausea.

During the past few weeks, I had groped desperately for some answer to my uncontrollable urge to drink, see other women, stay out all night. Something inside me wouldn't let go, though, and all the vows I'd made were useless. I'd just go right on with the same kind of behavior. But during these weeks, as I sought answers, I'd run across the name of Alcoholics Anonymous.

Still miserable when I left for work that morning, leaving Loris and the children still clinging restlessly to sleep, I made up my mind I wasn't coming home again if I had to come back in this condition.

Somehow, I struggled through the routine of work,

trying to hide my feelings. About ten in the morning, when I had a short break, I decided what I was going to do.

Shakily, I dialed Alcoholics Anonymous. "I'd like to make an appointment," I said.

Chapter 8

"Sweet Lelani" softly filled the airliner; a stewardess wearing a lei stopped with a tray of drinks beside two men. The older of the pair ran a manicured hand through his close-cropped grey hair. "I see you're awake."

"Huh? Oh, yeah." The other man, slim, in his mid-twenties, shook his head groggily. "That champagne take-off from L.A. knocked me out. I'd had a rough day."

"Well, as a doctor, perhaps I could suggest something—"

"So, you're a doctor?" Cook said. "Well, say, that's a coincidence. I just recently got out of the Air Force. I was a medic. A corpsman. Don Cook."

The older man showed rekindled interest. "Very happy to meet you." He offered his hand. "I'm Lawrence Rutgers. I'm a surgeon. I've been taking a bit of a holiday tour—San Francisco, Los Angeles, Honolulu. Haven't had a vacation in years; thought it high time I put my cares behind me. I suppose you could tell from my accent I'm from Canada."

"I noticed immediately. You see, I've been around . . . California, Oklahoma, Arkansas, Tennessee, *Alaska*."

"Alaska? Well—"

Cook interrupted again. "That experience with the medics was really worthwhile. I think I may go full scale into medicine. Perhaps specialize. Right now, I'm taking a holiday, too. To get my head . . . well, you know, to make up my mind. Dad said, 'Here, Son. A couple of thousand dollars ought to do you just about right. Get yourself a change of scenery.' "

A couple of thousand. Cook felt exhilarated. That part of it, at least, was true. He...*I*...had two thousand dollars in the overnight bag on the shelf.

It was, as a matter of fact, Don Cook Musgraves—and Tom Cook Collins—sitting there beside new friend, Dr. Rutgers, on a flight to Honolulu. Since taking off, I had been playing the role of Don Cook so well I'd forgotten my real identity. Just what I *wanted* to do.

The money talk brought back something of what had happened—and what hadn't happened. I *hadn't* kept my appointment with Alcoholics Anonymous. A few minutes after calling AA, I'd changed my mind.

Instead, I decided that I would—well, just be someone else, change my identity. I'd get out from under a horrible load of responsibility and guilt—guilt about what I was doing to Loris and the kids.

At first I wasn't conscious of planning to become an imposter. I was just trying to become someone else, because whatever Don *Musgraves* had become was a total failure.

I was convinced I wouldn't solve the alcohol problem, but I could be someone else with the same problem, and I knew it would involve crime of some kind.

There was a lot involved in planning the caper. Around noon I'd made up my mind I had to do it all in one day. I didn't want to have to go home again.

First of all, where would I go? To the farthest place I could and still be in the United States—Hawaii.

As for the money—I had the keys to the safe. I was in charge of it! Because the concession at North American was automated, there was only a handful of people around.

I got some masking tape from my secretary and told her and the head cashier, Nancy, to take extra time for lunch. I got paper bags from the storeroom, then went downstairs to the safe. I took off my shirt. Working fast, I scooped money into the bags and taped them around my thin chest—shrunken from dissipation, from not eating despite all the food around me.

Putting my shirt and jacket back on, I left the building, passing a lot of aircraft workers I'd come to know on sight. The guard at the gate, who knew me—yet, didn't really know me—said, "Leaving early?"

I was supremely confident. A skinny 135 pounds and wearing a jacket I'd bought when I'd weighed fifteen or twenty pounds more, I knew the loot was well concealed. No bulges. "Chester's taking over for me," I lied. "You have a good day now."

All so easy!

On the way to Los Angeles International Airport I stopped in a luggage store and bought a suitcase and an overnight bag, then a clothing store where I scooped up a supply of clothing.

In a gas station rest room, I changed. Back in the car, I packed my dirty laundry in the suitcase.

The money, I stuffed into the overnight bag. I'd just finished when the service station attendant came around the corner and saw my car parked near the rest room. "Stalled?" he inquired.

"No, just using the john."

He gave the suitcase and overnight bag on the back seat an eyeballing.

I froze.

But he turned on his heel, and went back to his office.

I was about to get into the driver's seat when, in a pile of trash near an alley, I saw a pair of levis and a shirt, bloodstains on the pants legs and shirt sleeves. An idea flashed. Looking around again, I hurried over and fished the items out of the trash.

I'd leave my car just outside the airport, with the dirty, bloody clothes in it. Sooner or later, it would be found—traced—and the story spread that I'd evidently met with foul play. A beautiful alibi so easily fabricated!

I parked along Sepulveda Boulevard, a few blocks from the underpass under the airport runway, left my keys in my unlocked car, carried the two pieces of luggage in either hand, and walked a couple of blocks. I glanced at my watch. Only fifteen minutes to get through the whole process of getting on that plane.

I waited two or three minutes for a cab to come by. None did. So I walked and practically ran the several blocks to the terminal.

Once aboard, I was Don Cook for sure.

But I was also tired. I had just enough energy to let the pretty blonde stewardess help me strap myself in, accept a glass of champagne, nod to the guy in the seat beside me, and fall off into crazy dreams. Exhilaration.

Actually, my dreams were seldom as crazy as my real life.

In a matter of six short hours, I had become $2,000 richer and, much more significant, Don Musgraves had vanished from the world. Don Cook, a discharged Air Force corpsman, was very much present.

A few hours later, we were approaching Honolulu.

Dr. Rutgers and I had been chatting warmly for quite a while, and I'd thrown around several medical terms which he seemed to consider accurate. "So you're quite a surgeon," I said. "That operation you described reminds me of an experience I had in, uh, Korea. The guy was dying and I either had to cut the slug out myself or let him die. No time to get a doctor flown in. I used my pocket knife. The guy lived."

"Remarkable!" Rutgers said.

We were quiet for a while; then he pulled out one of the plane's brochures and pointed to the name of a hotel. "That's where I'll be staying—The Princess Kaiulani."

"Is that so? That's a coincidence. That's where I'm staying."

"You don't say?"

"I *do* say." Up until now, I hadn't even given a thought to what I'd do once I got in Honolulu. I'd done a good, fast job of short-range planning, but hadn't thought beyond that.

We landed before midnight and I rode with Dr. Rutgers in the airline's limousine to the hotel, swankier even than it had appeared in the brochure. I knew the tab would be steep, but I was living it up.

I did have fears as I approached the desk. What if all the rooms were taken? What if they wouldn't let me have a room without a reservation? I had deliberately stalled until Dr. Rutgers had gone to the desk to pick up his reservation, but he didn't go up immediately. Sitting in a chair he was looking through a newspaper. If he saw me turned away by the clerk, he might become suspicious. After all, I had implied I had a reservation. Or . . . had I? I couldn't quite remember what I'd told him. I was in luck. There was a room for me at the inn.

The next week and a half was one mad whirl. Honolulu probably had more expensive, flashy night clubs per square mile than any other city in the world.

I was usually smacked out in my hotel room until evening, wrenched with pain, my head feeling twice its size.

I went to almost all the night spots played up in the tourist literature, and spent a fortune in cab fare alone.

One night, as I sat in the Kahili Bar of my hotel, almost broke, a lady in her fifties, wearing a loud, splashy muu-muu, slid onto the stool beside me and ordered a tikihaliki. She paid the bartender with a twenty-dollar bill and left the change on the bar. She started sipping her drink then turned to me. "You look as though you might be part Hawaiian. Your eyes have kind of a primitive look."

"As a matter of fact," I said, "my father was born on the island of Hawaii. I grew up in California, though. I've been here only a couple of weeks. I guess blood will tell."

"I'm already so excited about the place, I've decided to live here."

I ordered another drink and asked the bartender to make it two. "So, you are going to be permanent, then?"

"Oh, yes. I contacted a realtor before flying over; I'm negotiating right now for the lease on a house."

"By the way," I said. "I happen to be an attorney. If you need anyone to look over your papers, I'll be happy to do that."

"Oh, you're an attorney? Are you opening an office here?"

"I don't know—yet. I'm on leave of absence from a partnership—"

"In California?"

"Yes. In Newport Beach."

"Say, I'd be happy if you looked over the lease papers.

On legal matters, I was never very good. Tell you what, er . . . what's your name?"

"Oh, I'm sorry. Cook. Don Cook."

"And I'm Darlene Witherspoon. I'm *so* happy I met you. Tell you what; why don't you have lunch with me tomorrow? I have an appointment. . ."

We made a date to meet at Lum's. When Yang, the Chinese realtor, showed up, I put on my most authentic attorney's face.

While Yang and Darlene chatted, I flipped through the papers. It might as well have been written in Chinese. My eyes found it difficult to focus on the fine print, after the load I'd taken on the night before when Darlene had called it a night and the piano bar had come alive. But I put on a good show and finally said in a firm voice, "These seem to be in order."

The house was a four-bedroom place on Diamond Head Road, on Waikiki Beach. When the realtor got up to go, I said, "Nice meeting you, Mr. Yang. Mrs. Witherspoon and I are going to have some more coffee, but we appreciate your having taken the time."

"Not so. It was my pleasure, please."

I poured Darlene another cup of coffee from a fancy silver pot. "Uh, if you'll pardon me . . . I noticed reading the lease papers, the house you're leasing has four bedrooms and, well, as far as you've told me, you'll be all alone. Won't you feel a little jittery all by yourself in a big place like that? An attractive lady like yourself. What I'm trying to say is, I'd be happy to share the expenses if there's something we can work out."

A couple of days later, fat-cat Don Cook moved into an elegant, sprawling mansion in one of the most exclusive areas on Waikiki Beach.

Darlene Witherspoon and I respected each other's privacy, and I had my own bedroom with a lavish private bath all my own, kitchen privileges, use of the living room when I wanted it—the works.

I had my own reasons for being pleased with the situation, and *she* got her kicks from being personally acquainted with a "brilliant" young California attorney on leave.

As far as actually practicing, I knew it was impossible, and my job was to stall with the excuse I'd have to pass the bar exam for the State of Hawaii, which I told Darlene was stiffer than almost anywhere and required months of preparation.

Meanwhile, while I might pretend I had money coming in by the bushel basket regularly from my partnership and investments, as a point of fact, I had to plan quickly for some steady income to pay my own way.

One of the few jobs open to all in Hawaii was bartending. Unfortunately, while I knew how to manage a bar, and how to drink a drink, I didn't know how to mix beverages.

I decided to take on a second identity. I enrolled in a bartenders' school The time flew by and I graduated with highest honors, being the fastest student in mixing drinks who'd ever gone through the school, making the highest score on the proficiency test, which required remembering a series of drinks, and pouring them in the right order while being timed. Unfortunately, they didn't count how many I could drink.

It made such an impression on the head of the school that we became fast friends. But I turned down his offer to be an instructor when I heard that, because the school was accredited, personnel had to be investigated by the FBI and other federal agencies. He promised to keep his ears open in case a regular bartender's job came to his attention.

While I was a student, I decided I was spending too much on taxi fares and I faced the problem of buying a car. While the registration deal wouldn't be any headache, I kept wondering what I'd do about a driver's license which would show the name of "Don Cook."

I'd be okay driving unless I got stopped and my driver's license examined. The first question the cop would ask would be, "Your driver's license is under the name of Don Musgraves, but your registration says Don Cook. Why?"

Musgraves ... if my real name had been Jones. ... But—"Oh, *Musgraves*," they would muse. "Wasn't there a Musgraves on the teletype from California a few weeks back? Disappeared ... along with two thousand dollars?"

Bingo!

Yes, it would be very wise to get a *new* driver's license for Don Cook.

In the neighborhood where I lived, I became acquainted with some high-class neighbors. Right next door were a couple from Australia, fair dinkum people named Percy and Lillian Thomas. When Percy found out I was a successful attorney from near Disneyland, he was really impressed. One day he invited me to meet some attorney friends who belonged to a cricket club. "Why don't you come along Sunday, mate?" he asked.

I bought some sneakers and, in a couple of days, went to the Honolulu Cricket Club and immediately became a member of the team.

Just as I'd caught on to the art of mixing drinks, I quickly caught on to cricket. A couple of weeks later, we beat the pants off the Queen of England's Guard Ship team, which was traveling around the world taking her Majesty to the members of the Commonwealth.

Now I was rubbing elbows with the really high-class people.

My acquaintance with these chaps helped impress others who might not be as high class, but who were, like me, looking for ways to make a buck or two.

However, I didn't wait for various schemes to bear fruit. I needed instant money. I learned of a printer, Hector Waliwali, who was starting up in business.

The first printing job Waliwali gave me was printing up payroll checks and, right away, I ripped off a couple of sheets with about a dozen blank checks altogether. I stuck them into my pocket for future reference. They were Hector's own company checks—WALIWALI HAWAII PRINTING.

Other than this, I played it cool and worked my way up until I was trusted enough to go to the bank on Friday afternoons with my employer's own check to cash, usually for $100 or $200. For weekend expenses, probably. I'd come back to the shop and count the money into his hand just to show him how honest I was.

Naturally, with my propensity for figuring the angles, I made it a point to become very friendly with all the tellers.

Now I was in a better position to apply for a driver's license.

Obtaining it, however, also required identification. I pondered how to swing this and remembered that while I was moving into my room at Darlene's house, I'd discovered some discharge papers belonging, presumably, to the former owner.

Changing my name hadn't changed my basic philosophy of life, which was "finders keepers."

I deliberately got behind on a big, rush printing job and was in the shop after closing time, when Tom Pepikalaki, the other printer's devil, and his boss had called it a day. I whipped out those discharge papers. Using a special printing process which made paper sensitive enough to alter writing, I flicked off the answers on the discharge papers and then typed in "Don Cook" and all the phony details, as fancy dictated, to such questions as "date and place of birth," "number of brothers and sisters," "occupation," "military specialty," etc.

Next day, at the Department of Motor Vehicles, I wrote a lot of lies on the application, paid the governor, passed the written test, and flunked the driver's test. "Sorry, buddy, try again in ninety days," the examiner said, handing me a temporary permit, worthless as far as bona-fide identification was concerned.

The sensible thing to do would be not to buy a car, just cool it for a while.

But whether I was going by the name of Musgraves or Cook, playing it cool for very long wasn't one of my strong points. I bought a beat-up old station wagon.

Tom Pepikalaki, my co-worker, and I got to be good drinking buddies. He didn't resent it that Waliwali trusted me with those Friday bank trips. He was a good-time, good-natured joe, and all he cared about on Fridays was collecting his own personal paycheck and proceeding to blow it on booze and broads until Monday morning. Just like me, actually. That's why we clicked.

A less honest pal got pretty excited when he heard that I hobnobbed with the nobs. He was Chuckie Tulikalari, whom I'd met at bartender's school. My connections inspired him to hatch a scheme to con rich people into investing in a South Sea Island paradise venture.

The idea was to get deposits of around $100 on a phony recreational development supposedly to involve a group of small, uninhabited islands near Tahiti.

"As an attorney," Tulikalari said, "you can handle the negotiations. I got me a job slinging drinks, and I meet a lot of shipping company big shots. I can drop a lot of names. You catch 'em."

More than two months back, when I'd first made the decision to become Don Cook and take off for Honolulu, I'd started up from the deepest trough of despair and had been lifted higher and higher, like a surfer who'd caught his wave just right and was riding high, rolling faster and faster toward the beach.

Immediately, I had slackened off somewhat on my drinking, knowing I had to keep my head clear for all the decisions my new life would demand.

But now the same old thing happened. At the very crest of the wave, just when I had to maintain my precarious balance most urgently, I went back to taking a shot or two of liquor every two or three hours during the day, to keep me going. I was getting shaky and nervous again, yet putting on a front of supreme self-confidence and common sense all the more, even to myself.

Tulikalari's plan sounded like a good way to rake in quick cash, and I didn't stop to check into anything. Instead, I agreed enthusiastically to every wild idea my fellow alcoholic suggested.

I took a big chance using Waliwali's printing press on the sly to print up the proposals, including actual photos of islands, glass-bottomed boats, sparkling coral sands, and swinging native girls.

"Man, that's a winner!" Tulikalari said, beaming, when we went over the literature in his messy hotel room. "Just remember, you've got to tap that cricket clique of yours. I'm doing my share, throwing names around. But you're the one who really swings the weight with your image as a sharpie lawyer from California."

I nodded, "Let's drink on it!"

Somehow, I managed to continue to walk a tightrope with Darlene. We continued respecting each other's individuality. More than that, I sensed that, being a newcomer to Honolulu herself, she eagerly welcomed the "in"

I gave her with upper-crust neighbors. She had the money to *buy* her way into the crowd, but she lacked the one ingredient to make her position complete: the glamour of a smooth-talking, outgoing mixer, which I supplied.

That was fine with Don Cook. I even brought girls in during the night to finish up a drinking bout and try to cap it off with more than drinks. In the few months I'd been in Hawaii, I'd picked up dozens of girls off the beach, in bars, downtown, anywhere.

As the wave beneath me began to wobble, I sought satisfaction in the opposite sex more and more with less and less pleasure.

Then one morning several telephone calls warned me that some of the investors in our shaky financial deal were getting impatient for solid news on the progress of the Island Resort Plan. My Hawaiian adventure had about ended.

The next day, something else hastened my decision to depart the Islands. After I'd finally gotten to sleep, after a hard day's night, someone banged on my door.

I jumped like a shot. Wobbling to the door, I opened it a crack. It was one of my attorney friends I'd met through the cricket club, a Chinese by the name of Wah We Wong. "Let me in." He seemed wild with excitement. I let him in. "Hey, you, Don!" he blurted out. "You know my pop he was appointed supreme court judge and I tell him all about you."

"Gee, thanks," I murmured.

"He so happy and want you go meet him."

"Uh, er, play that over again, Wah We. Why . . . why would he want to meet *me*?" Was this his way of saying they suspected I was a quack lawyer? Or that the lid had blown off the island caper?

"Oh, he can help you pass that bar exam chop-chop! He want see you very soon, thank you."

"Oh, well, let me have a little time to look at my calendar," I murmured. I was relieved I was not already in the barbecue pit; at the same time, I knew it was imminent, because there's nothing like spilling your guts to a supreme court judge to pull your cover if you're posing as an attorney.

The only thing to do was—up, up and away.

But I had drunk up my printer's wages the minute the money had come off the press.

However, I did have a number of blank checks with WALIWALI HAWAII PRINTING printed boldly at the top, *and* people at the bank knew me as an honest, hard-working employee of said firm—*who* regularly came in Friday afternoons just before closing time and cashed checks from $100 upwards, checks which cleared beautifully.

I made reservations for a flight the following Saturday to San Francisco, knowing I'd have a grace period because the banks were closed over the weekend. Then, Friday afternoon—"Mr. Waliwali needs a *couple* of checks cashed this time, Sylvia," I told the teller, smiling my ingratiating smile and winking. "One for $100 and one for, let's see"—I glanced down at the check—"$500."

When I got back to the shop to wind up business for the day, I handed over the $100 in cash to Waliwali, carefully counting it into his palm. I kept the $500. It was going to take me away from the Hawaiian Supreme Court.

Chapter 9

Alcohol was oozing out of me in beads of sweat as I veered erratically from one lane to another crossing the Oakland Bay Bridge. All I was aware of, besides acute discomfort, was a collage of whiskey bottles, dollar signs, yellow lines on black pavement, and arrows pointing in all directions of the compass, especially *down*.

I was frantic to get away, as far away as I could, anywhere. At the moment, I felt as though the only thing I'd left in San Francisco was several hundred dollars and a trail of empty bottles.

The shiny new 1963 rented Chevie couldn't make up its mind which lane to stay in. "You're the boss, boy," a voice kept echoing in my skull. "Which way is it to be? Inland? Across the valley and on to Reno? Ah! Big money there, boy."

But the picture popping into my mind was one I'd seen on billboards everywhere so many times: a girl in scanty clothes serving drinks, and the words HAROLD's CLUB ... LAS VEGAS ...WHERE FRIENDLY PEOPLE MEET.

Okay. It would be the desert.

I was on my way to Vegas on a business trip. The details of the business could be worked out on the way.

Then—Las Vegas was everything I had imagined. By the time I got there, the sky was dark. Las Vegas itself was lit up like a Christmas tree. Christmas in May!

Each place tried to be bigger and better than the other. Each one boasted it had something different to offer. I checked into a motel and started out to see for myself.

The classier the place, the more sophisticated the girls tried to look. I wasn't too discriminating. I gave them all the eye.

I took in a dozen gambling spots, trying to cram everything into one night, trying to avoid thinking, darting in and out of places thronged with people trying to laugh.

I still had some of those fifty dollar bills left, and they were searing holes in my pocket.

Once I stopped gambling, I realized how tired I was. I'd only lost ten dollars. But I was bored. And lonely.

In the motel room, I kept seeing the hard faces of the girls in the clubs. Some of them were just *barely* out of their teens.

Without undressing, I flopped down on the bed; and Jo Ann, the cocktail waitress in San Francisco, coalesced out of the kaleidoscope the bright lights were turning in my brain.

Was I running away from Jo Ann? Seeking in Vegas a way to turn her off? Why Jo Ann? She was just another girl I'd lied to in a dimly lit bar.

The sun, shining in my face, woke me up four hours later. I'd forgotten to pull the drapes. I left the motel and went to one of those places serving breakfast any old time of day.

Most of the waitresses wore their masks of cheerfulness, but the customers around me look worried and dreary, resting up between losing streaks.

Musgraves the Mouth didn't feel like talking to anyone. As I was leaving the restaurant, trying not to jiggle my stomach too much, I caught a glimpse of myself in the mirror. I hadn't even shaved. My clothes had had a rough sleep the night before. I looked as crummy as I felt.

On the way back to the motel, I saw a display of firearms in a pawn shop window. I studied the display, then focussed on a .38 New Colt revolver. Something seemed to raise that gun right up off its pad.

The long-faced old man inside told me it was mine for $35. All I had to do was sign a card for it. But he didn't carry ammo. I drove around town for almost two hours, trying various gun shops, before finding one that stocked the right cartridges.

I went back to the motel room, the gun in a paper

bag, then sat on the bed and began to load it. I wasn't really sure why I'd bought it or what I'd do with it.

I could kill myself. Of course, a few things were left that I hadn't done yet. Still, I'd had a good sampling of everything. I was on a downhill slide, and it would be a good time to do something like this, some final act . . .

I'd started on that downhill slide in Hawaii. Then the fast take-off and flying 38,000 feet high in the air, nursing a hangover from weeks of drinking—that had nothing to do with anything, did it?

Once I had landed in San Francisco, I had made a valiant effort to climb back up. A good time might be the cure. I asked a cabbie where a fellow found all the fun around town.

"North Beach," he answered as he whirled around out of the San Francisco Airport. "I'll take you there." He had me pegged real quick. "You in for the convention?"

That was my cue. "I just flew in from Honolulu. I'm looking for smart, high-class, good-looking girls to send to Hawaii as waitresses." I winked.

"I get the message."

"So, if you'll suggest a good hotel on the way, you can drop me there and come back in an hour to show me North Beach."

He had guessed my tastes, and I was more than satisfied with the hotel he chose. Later, on the way to North Beach, I tried to relax. I fought against the sickness that had laid me out in flight.

North Beach. I hadn't seen anything like it before. You could go into one bar after another and find something unique. There were bars for both male and female homosexuals. In one where the "ladies" went, butches were easy to spot—gals in blue jeans, checkered shirts, close-cropped hair.

By eleven o'clock, I was smacked. I impressed a waitress when I ordered another drink and paid for it with a fifty-dollar bill. I counted out the change carefully, tipped her well, then left the balance carelessly on the table, as though it was just a pile of scrap paper.

It lit lights—in eyes.

"Say, where does a guy see something different in this town?" I teasingly asked the waitress.

"Why don't you stick around and I'll show you," she answered. "I'm Jo Ann."

I'd been eyeballing her for quite some time. Now I'd made my pitch. And she struck up a deal. I liked this one. She was the best-looking girl in the place. There was something arresting about her hair—kind of dark with streaks of white making her look even younger than she was.

"I'll stick around till closing time," I said.

Jo Ann turned out to be a terrific tour guide. She knew all the after-hours, the ones that serve liquor in coffee cups after two o'clock and go right on as if there weren't closing hours anywhere.

The entertainment was better in these places, and I threw fifty-dollar bills around as though they were kites.

The next day Jo Ann asked me to come along to a couple of parties. I rented a car and we hit a couple of topless places, just opening up around that time. We played "Can you top this?"

As part of Jo Ann's tour, she introduced me to some of her friends and, to show them how affluent and important I was, I bought the drinks. Inspired by this, they invited us to a whole round of parties. The next few days was a continuous whirl, a merry-go-round where you reached for a cocktail glass instead of the brass ring.

I renewed my car rental agreement for another couple of days to take Jo Ann to a party out in Mill Valley—a real swinging affair in a swanky home. We were not displeased when the host offered to put us up for the night, or what was left of it.

When I took Jo Ann home, she wondered why I was so quiet. I couldn't really explain it. I didn't know myself. I just felt washed out, aching and feeble. I was nervous and restless and wanted to be alone. Something seemed to be pulling on me.

Jo Ann was pulling on me. She made it difficult to drive. "Why can't I stay at your place today?" She turned my head and kissed me and wouldn't let go. I nearly hit someone head on.

"I don't feel like anything right now," I mumbled, finally managing to yank my head away and tighten my grip on the wheel.

After I'd dropped her off, I went back to my hotel and tried to sleep. The walls of the hotel room seemed to be closing in. Every noise from the street made me jump. I had to get out.

Well, why not? I had the car. If I didn't return it tomorrow, they'd just assume I wanted it longer. Of course, I hadn't told them I'd take it on any long trips.

But, who cared, anyway?

All these things flashed through my mind as I toyed with my gun in the Las Vegas motel room. I kept trying to figure out why I'd had the feeling about things closing in on me. Why did I have to drink and drink and drink until my body was convulsed in pain? Who was I, anyway? What was I doing here? Why had I messed up my life? What was the use of going on with it, the bold, hard thrusts—then the let-downs and self-recrimination and escaping?

I stared dumbly at the gun, getting the feel of it, learning its contours. I sat there, putting bullets in, taking them out—putting them in, taking them out. I aimed it at a calendar on the door and wondered if I could kill Time.

Then I aimed at a chair. Then at my head.

"No," I said. "No, I'll wait and see what happens. I'll have one more try at Oklahoma State. Then . . ."

I'd decided to go to Stillwater and see if the university was still there. If anything in this world had stood still and remained the same, if some place Don Musgraves could find himself, if a place waited for him somewhere. . . .

Along the way, I discovered I was low on money. If I cooled it, I had enough; but I didn't like doing it this way. The gun lay on the seat beside me. Why didn't I do something with it?

I stopped at a motel, tucked the gun under my belt, put on my bright red jacket to cover it. There should be some cash in the office.

Although if my bluff were called, I probably wouldn't have the guts to shoot anyone, unless I ended up killing myself. Still, something inside me instinctively knew how to pull off an armed robbery, almost as if someone were programming me as I sat there in the car, eyeing that motel office.

The entrance to the office was on the side. I headed for the door, then stopped, a force seeming to stay my footsteps even before my eye took in the scene. Two children were playing with little cars on the floor inside the office.

The door was open, welcoming me. The kids were racing the cars back and forth and laughing when the cars hit each other. I rehearsed what I would say as I stood in the doorway, looking, listening.

Something caught at my throat. I was feeling sick again. My knees buckled and I almost fell. Somewhere in the back of my mind, I heard a baby crying.

I turned quickly and almost ran, stumbling back to the car to sink down in the seat, trying not to think, trying to block out everything.

Before reaching Stillwater, I phoned in for a reservation at the Campus Hotel, near the U, catering to executives and academic people. The place had a lot of prestige and status.

When I arrived I was quite a while removing all the dirt and grime of traveling, and putting on my "executive" clothes. It was harder getting that look back on my face. Something must be wrong with the mirror. It was telling lies. The skin on my face was stretched taut, the bags under my eyes stood out, my complexion was pasty, sallow. Who was this staring back at me?

Actually, Stillwater and the university looked pretty much the same. But I didn't see one familiar face, not even in the coffee shop, where I'd known almost everyone.

I had a great story to tell someone: I had decided

I would tell all my friends, and *their* friends, I was a trouble-shooter for a large chain of restaurants in Hawaii.

But I couldn't find anyone to whom I could tell my story.

Finally, as I was about to give up, I saw Professor Duncan, one of my former instructors. I walked up and pushed out my hand. "Hi, Prof. Remember me?"

He seemed a bit distracted.

"Musgraves. Don Musgraves."

"Are you one of my students?" He scratched his head. Then he grinned in an embarrassed way. "Oh, of course. Musgrooves." He looked at his watch. "Dear me. I'm terribly sorry. I'm late for my next class. Perhaps later?"

Why hadn't he asked me to give a little talk to his class?

Looking around, memories flooded. The buildings were there. The people were gone. Time had receded, like a tide.

"This place stinks," I blurted out. I turned and jumped into my rented Chevie.

"I know someone who'll remember me."

I was thinking of my Army buddy, Vern Greenwood. I knew where his mother lived, way up in Illinois. Just a day and a half of fast driving.

Stillwater didn't seem to notice I had left. When I got behind the wheel and out onto the two-lane highway, I patted the gun in my belt and felt as though I were somebody, after all.

So what if I didn't have more than a few dollars left? I could take care of that.

Vern's mother remembered me. She invited me in to have lunch and we visited.

She told me Vern was teaching high school in another small town nearby and gave me the address. Somehow, she didn't seem too happy about Vern.

Vern was glad to see me, but he didn't seem much better off than I was. He was trapped in a small town and had done some things he wasn't too proud of. He was still a heavy drinker.

"You make me feel better, knowing you're doing so

great," Vern said, trying to look cheerful. "Imagine that, a big shot executive, head of a chain of restaurants in *Hawaii*. I always knew you'd make it. Listen, Don, why don't we forget *my* troubles. Let's just have a ball while you're here."

"Yeah, well, I was going to that big restaurant convention in Chicago, but even if I get there a day late, it's no big thing."

It made me feel good that Vern, at least, was convinced I was *something*, that he looked up to me.

We did just that—had a ball. But there was one problem: I had to back up my big words with big money. One day while Vern was teaching, and we were scheduled for a bash that night, I peeked into my billfold. It stared back vacantly.

A liquor store in an adjoining town looked as if it might be an easy touch. I was going to try it in broad daylight, and something inside me said, "Go ahead, boy. Don't worry. You can do it." The same voice guided me all along the way. It all came naturally, just sauntering in as though I were a customer, the gun safely hidden. I grabbed the first piece of merchandise I came to, a loaf of Russian Rye, then went to the counter and wrote out a note on the inside of a cigarette wrapper: PUT THE MONEY IN A SACK AND YOU WON'T GET HURT.

It worked like a charm the very first time! The guy looked at me with a brief, appraising glance and, as soon as I motioned to the bulge under my jacket, he moved—but fast.

I walked slowly, kind of sideways, out of the store, then down the street, only a little shaky because it had happened so fast—and so easily. Once around the corner, I removed my bright red jacket, put it under the seat, and drove off—slowly.

Just as I pulled into the main street, I was passed by four patrol cars racing toward the liquor store.

I felt better than I had for weeks. I was somebody again.

Vern and I lived it up for the next week, going out to night clubs, dancing, sitting around talking and reminiscing about our Army days and the big jumps we had made, the fights we had had, the girls we had met.

Whenever we met girls in bars, I'd give them my line about being sent by a big Honolulu restaurant and night club group to find girls to train as waitresses. The Midwestern farmers' daughters and small town girls on the loose, who'd dreamed of exotic adventures, were really fascinated. They gave me anything I wanted just to "be considered," and I wanted only one thing from all of them.

I couldn't go on much longer pretending to be self-confident and zestful when all the time I was burning up inside, the alcohol dissolving my cells, twisting my stomach, vibrating my skull every time I tried to think. Not that I was thinking much these days.

I finally had to end my visit with Vern, and started off for Chicago. In Chicago, I looked around for a bank to rob. But I hadn't figured on all banks having armed guards. I spent a day driving from one bank to another, going in and out, trying to find one without guards. Somewhere along the line, it occurred to me that robbing a bank would be a federal rap.

Instead, I headed for a small town and tried a liquor store again.

"I suppose you want my wallet, too?" the clerk asked. "I've only been robbed twice in the past year and this makes it a *charm*," he added sarcastically.

As I drove out of town, I asked myself why I hadn't taken the guy's wallet, after all. It must have had the bulk of the money in it, because the bag only had about $200. I could have had his credit cards, too, and stuff I might be able to use for identification.

From there, I headed west. Something was pulling me downhill. No matter how frantically I whipped my legs, I couldn't climb back up. I'd been aware at Vern's of my face caving in, new lines every day. Lately, it had been agony even to try to smile. My mouth had a downward cast, hung partly open showing my stained uneven teeth. I looked like a guy in a Dracula movie turning into a werewolf.

The gun gave me brief feelings of power, just like

the speed I started popping gave me momentary periods of calm, but the dark tide was too powerful to keep back for long.

Given my never-ending thirst for liquor and the reckless way I spent money, by the time I reached St. Louis, I was low again in more ways than one. It was dusk and I was ready to crawl into fresh sheets and die.

But being close to broke bugged me. Before holing up, I decided to pull a job. I picked a liquor store at random, walked in, took a jar of pickles off the shelf, and put it down on the counter. It wasn't until I handed the guy the note that I noticed another couple. It was too late—the guy saw my hesitation and he started to hesitate. I had to act decisively.

"That note's no joke," I said grimly. "Just keep cool or you'll be sorry. So will they." I said it low, but the authority in my voice surprised even me. I was desperate and it almost seemed that someone else was in command. I'd never said things like that, even in fun—yet I sounded like I'd been talking that way all my life.

Still, my hand shook violently while it rested on the gun in my belt. I knew the guy was giving me the once-over so he could describe me to the cops. His eyes jumped from my face to my bright red jacket to my T-shirt, dropped to my jeans, then up again to get another fix on the color of my eyes and hair.

Maybe the red jacket would throw them when they looked for me. I instinctively had affected it because it stood out so much that, once I'd removed it, I'd be even less conspicuous.

I made quite a haul in that store, several hundred dollars, and I decided I would have some fun no matter how lousy I felt. I found a lively cocktail lounge with a loud piano bar and decided to rent the place for the night. For some reason, the chicks I sat next to, after looking at me in response to my wry comments, edged away. "I'm trying to find some swinging chicks for movie extras," I told one girl. This stopped her for a little while.

I ended up the evening spilling my guts all over the floor and they shipped me out onto the street.

Sick, lonely, exhausted, I wound my way to my car and drove back to my motel room. Something kept echoing in my head—a voice. Jo Ann's. She was the only person since my return from Honolulu who had really noticed me, made me feel important. I phoned her long distance.

"I'm coming back, baby," I said.

"Don! Honey! What happened to you?"

"It's a long story," I said. "Maybe I'll tell you sometime."

"Honey, I was afraid something bad had happened to you. So, well, don't get mad at me, but I went down to that car rental place to see when you were scheduled to return the car. You know what they said? You'd run off with it. They have a warrant out . . ."

Even though I had unconsciously known they would have a warrant out on me, still, it gave me a jolt.

"Aaahhh, Jo Ann, baby. There's a big mistake somewhere. Honest. Someone's really feeding you a line. Don't let it bug you, baby. I'll be in town Friday for sure and we'll just forget I was ever gone."

I hung up. Hearing her voice, a momentary elation lifted me, but then I crumpled in tears.

I planned to rip off more money on the way back. You don't last long on the fun circuit in San Francisco unless you're stashed. I hit two more liquor stores. In one place, there was a regular little talkathon going between the man and woman behind the counter and a couple who were getting groceries and six packs.

I was in too much of a hurry, too strung out to back down just because of complications. I guess I didn't care whether I was caught or not. I was tired. Dead tired. I plunked a bottle of wine down on the counter, thrust the note at the guy. All he did was laugh!

I looked around. The clerk showed the note to his two customers and then to his wife. They all laughed. "Can I get you a cup of black coffee?" the lady asked in a pleasant tone. "Might help you sober up."

I stepped back so all were in front of me, and pulled out my gun. "This ain't 'Can You Top This,' " I croacked.

The guy's adam's apple bobbed like he was going to

spit it out. Then, never taking his eyes off the shaking barrel of the gun, he felt his way to the cash register and dropped everything into a bag his wife held out for him—a bag with St. Vitus' Dance.

I got out fast.

I was furious! I'd taken enough there, but I wanted to hit a few more just for spite. If anyone gave me any lip, I might even use the gun. To have been forced to go the whole way, the gun out, and all that bit, tore me up. Now I was after revenge.

I gathered up enough stuff in the second store for a good snack to last a while on the road and had the girl bag it. While she did so, and rang it up on the register, I glanced coolly around. She was alone, all right, and just old enough to be working in a liquor store.

This one ought to be easy, after all. I'd be gentle with this one—even apologetic. She could have been a kid sister. Even before I spread the note out on the counter, she was staring at my face, her pale blue eyes wide, puzzled. She swallowed and licked her lips.

Then in the mirror behind her I could see why. I looked like an escapee from Forest Lawn Cemetery.

"Don't worry, honey. I won't hurt you. Just hand over the money, I'll just tuck it in with the groceries. I won't hurt you, honest."

She seemed paralyzed. I thought I'd better hurry her up, kid gloves or not. I pulled my jacket open to show her the butt of the gun nestling under my belt.

She gasped, then started to weep.

I couldn't help looking at her eyes. The fear was real. She thought I was going to kill her. Nothing in the hard lines of my decaying face told her any differently.

Her fright really shook me. She saw something in me that I hadn't seen—even in that mirror. She saw I was capable of taking someone's life, that I was a killer.

I made it out of there on the double, with the money, forgetting to walk slowly, forgetting to remove my jacket until I'd gotten into the car and had already driven five blocks.

I drove straight through town, stopping only for red lights, steeling myself not to look down the side streets. A cop passed me, going the other way.

My idea was to put as many miles between myself and that girl as I could, The farther I could get away from her, the better I would feel. I thought.

It didn't work that way.

The girl haunted me. Her eyes followed me—all the way.

Chapter 10

I stood on the slight slope, supporting my weight with one hand against a tall pine, and looked out across a deep, jagged canyon, filling my lungs with clear, pine-scented air.

What peace! Across the canyon, the sun touched the tips of millions of pine needles on forested slopes, a green mantle frosted with silver.

I dug into my pockets for cigarette makings. This had to be heaven!

A loud, sharp bark interrupted me. "Musgraves! What the tarnation you think you're doing?" I heard the heavy boots crashing through underbrush. "Get back to that pick! You're supposed to keep up with the line, or did you forget?"

I turned around and smiled. "I just took off to answer a call of nature. I'll catch up okay."

Frank, the guard, snorted. "Don't stray so far again. People might get ideas."

When I returned to the line hacking away at the rocky soil along the ridge, and hoisted my heavy pick, Red looked over and grinned. "Dreaming again, Musgraves? Where were you this time—in Vegas?"

I came down hard with my pick. "Not out here, man. Out here, you don't have to dream a thing. It's in the barracks after supper when things get boring."

Pedro hollered, "That's when I miss the senoritas, on the cold night when the moon shines in those cracks in the walls, man. Brrr!" He hunched his shoulders. "Then ees when you need the hah-nee to cuddle up with and make the loving."

"Pedro," Red snickered, "you been in and out of camp and jail so long, you forgot what a broad is like."

"If you'd stay out of L.A.," I said, "get busted down in Tijuana, I hear they let chicks visit you in the jails in Mexico."

"Filthy place," Pedro spat. "Sure. That one thing, very okay. But too many cockroaches!"

"Cockroaches? You ever been in the Lincoln Heights Jail?" Red asked.

"Would you guys care to be transferred back?" Frank's voice was calm and authoritative. "Musgraves, you could be the first to go back, you know. You're rocking this boat. Would you men like to be up here after dark? This fire line's got to go down to those rocks before anyone goes anywhere." He shrugged. "But, suit yourselves. It's no skin off my teeth. I can always be relieved."

"Hey, Frankie," Pedro said. "You wouldna make us miss our beans and tortillas, eh?"

After Frank had gone off, Red chortled. "He always picks on the quietest one. Huh! You're just two feet back of the main line and he has hemorrhages."

Pedro leaned on his pick and looked at me. "How you know? Maybe Musgraves really screw it up for us, like Frankie say. But I guess you donkeys no care. Poor Don Juan, he no do nothing wrong. Big hero!"

I gave Pedro a glare and hit the ground hard again. Splinters of rock zinged against tree trunks.

I worked mechanically, easily making up for lost time. The wonderful, uplifted feeling from my communion in the trees; the zest from good exercise and mountain air, the new world I was creating in my mind—all served to make me buoyant and forgiving.

I was a new man! This honor camp was really rehabilitating me. I weighed more than I had in years, my muscles bulged like Superman's, and all my senses were alert to everything around me—except when I let my mind drift off into the bright future which would begin soon.

Most of all, I had recently made a discovery that was going to transform Don Musgraves once and for all, to make him a person who would actually deserve *Loris* and who, in a few months, would start to make it up to her for all the torment and misery I had caused her and the children.

My body worked rhythmically as my mind trailed off to reconstruct what had led to this miraculous change . . .

After my wild spree of stick-ups, sick but functioning on nervous energy, driven by something inside of me pulling all the strings, I arrived back in San Francisco. I had my car washed, then parked it in front of the rental agency just before it was due to open.

Later, from a public phone booth, I called the agency and represented myself as an attorney calling in behalf of Don Musgraves, informing them a hotel doorman was supposed to have returned the car several weeks ago.

The manager of the agency had to admit the car was, as a matter of fact, parked right out in front of the lot.

I called Jo Ann and suggested she come over to my hotel. "I just got back and we can make some plans for the weekend," I said.

I was cleaned up, looking like a half-way civilized human being, when she came in. We talked a while, throwing around ideas as to how we could make up for lost time. When I opened my attache case to grab a wad of money, my gun fell out.

She gave a little gasp. "Don, just what *do* you do for a living?" She sounded worried.

I put the gun back and snapped the case shut. "Jo Ann, honey," I said in a grave voice. "I've been postponing telling you this but, all along, I knew some day I would have to. Quite frankly—well, I work for the C.I.D.—"

"What's *that*?" she said with a little shiver, as though I'd mentioned the Mafia.

"The Counter Intelligence Department," I said grimly. "Don't spread this around, I'm trusting you." It was hard not to come out with a devilish laugh. I'd really reached out, but it was certainly a good cover. Posing as a secret agent, I could do virtually anything and explain it away as my normal routine. I should have thought of it sooner.

Jo Ann was duly impressed and wanted to hear all about it.

"Sorry, baby. I shouldn't have told you that much."

"But I won't tell anyone, darling," she persisted.

Ever since we'd met again, coming together in a tight embrace, Jo Ann's rich, moist lips tasting so good after my long, lonely trip across the United States, I had detected in our relationship something I hadn't quite realized was there when I'd taken off.

Jo Ann acted as though she really liked me, more than all the girls I'd been shacking up with and getting drunk with since running off from Loris and my other life.

"Don . . . Don. I—. You really turn me on. I want to know everything there is to know about you."

"You turn me on, too, baby." I kissed her—hard, hungrily. As shallow as she was and as briefly as I'd known her, she was a warm light in a cold darkness. "But, I just can't. Let's get started on that weekend."

A couple of hours later, during the late afternoon, after a few drinks in a bar in San Francisco's North side, I finally gave her a cock and bull story about a shaky character I was shadowing. She bought it and even paid the sales tax.

During the next three days, I spent more than five hundred dollars on booze, bennies, and good times. Jo Ann and I would meet people in bars and set up parties. I ended up paying the tabs and drank myself into a stupor. I dropped dozens of speed pills. I hardly knew what I was doing. Vaguely, I did feel I was sliding down, down, down into a bottomless black pit of drink, drugs, and dissipation.

On Tuesday morning, I woke up half-way sober, desperately sick, and broke.

I was sick. I had no money. But I still had that gun. Suicide? Make an end to the whole, stupid scene? This phony flitting around in the hulks of other people's identities?

I looked at the gun. How about pulling some more stick-ups? I pondered it. Then I decided that, at the rate

I was going, I'd probably end up killing someone. Anyway, I was too shaky to pull it off.

Too ill to get a job, pull a robbery, and too cowardly to kill myself. Only one thing left to do—give myself up.

If I phoned Jo Ann, she might talk me out of leaving. Anyway, I didn't want to talk to anyone. I scribbled out a telegram telling her I had to be going again—the man I was tracking was on the move.

I was in a daze when I got off in Los Angeles twelve hours later. In a phone booth, I called the police. "I'm giving myself up. Come and get me." I told them about lifting the money from *the Downey* plant, even admitting I'd run off to Hawaii. But I was vague on everything else. I wasn't about to tell them anything at all about the liquor store jobs. The North American deal was bad enough. I was interested in a rest stop, not getting sent up for fifty years.

I was stunned at the reaction. "Sorry, we can't pick you up," the guy said. "We've no warrant for you."

After pleading, I managed to get them to come and get me anyway. Riding to the station in the squad car, they laughed and joked about not having anything on me. I wasn't even drunk now. Just sick. Dying inside.

After further discussion at the station and a dozen phone calls, the mystery was finally solved. The North American Aviation plant where I'd stolen the money was in Downey—and Downey was in Los Angeles *County* territory. While they processed me for transfer to county authorities, I went through further agonies.

By the time I was driven to the Downey police department and went through more grilling, I was practically dead. They had to carry me into jail, I sacked out on the concrete floor of the drunk tank.

For two days, I was interviewed periodically. Finally the investigating officers concluded they weren't sure what they'd do with me! "North American has withdrawn charges," the detective announced.

"What does that mean?" I asked.

"They won't prosecute. But, California law says, even if the complainant withdraws charges, the D.A. can prosecute. The problem is, the D.A. wants some time to make up his mind." He grunted. "Actually, he suggested letting you go."

"But I don't want to go," I protested.

"Well, he said we should release you in the custody of your wife."

"My *wife*? Oh, God! Loris? I don't want to face her."

The detective shrugged. "That's what the D.A. wants."

When Loris showed up, I faced her, all right—faced the music—a real funeral dirge. I sat across from her in that dick's office. I hadn't shaved or bathed for four days. I was shaky and could only mumble. The detective looked at Loris, then at me and said, "Musgraves! Man, you got to be nuts. To pull the things you did and have a wife like you got."

I knew it was the truth.

Loris had no intention of taking me to her parents' house where she was living. We agreed I'd stay at my folks' place, despite my extreme reluctance. My parents had moved to Orange County from Oklahoma while I was on my imposter trip.

The day after I had caught the plane to Honolulu, the police had shown up at the apartment and informed Loris that the safe at the place where I'd worked had been robbed and I hadn't reported for work. They were virtually certain I had ripped off the money.

Loris was really shaken. She honestly had no idea where I'd gone, though she mentioned Las Vegas because I was always talking about going there. She was in a state of near shock for several days. She knew she had to tell her parents, and mine, but she kept putting off this horrible task. When she finally brought herself to it, her parents retorted with the old "I told you so" bit.

It nearly killed *my* parents. Mom was convinced I was dead, especially after my car, with the blood-stained clothes I'd planted, had been found.

My dad was absolutely crushed. All his life, he'd expounded his philosophy of "work hard, keep your nose clean, and you can write your own ticket." He'd tried to teach us kids the wisdom of honesty and fair play.

Loris told me she missed me and still loved me. I couldn't see how! "I'd look up at the stars at night," she said, "and wonder, 'Where are you, my darling?'"

My oldest child, Mike, was three years old when I'd taken off and he was old enough to ask about Daddy. When Loris cried, he would ask her, "Are you crying about Daddy?" She could only nod. What else could she do? What can you say to a three-year-old? "Your old man's a drunken crook?"

Before we arrived at my parents' house, Loris and I agreed to think about things for a while, then talk on the phone about what to do. She went into my parents' house with me but stayed only a few minutes. When she left, things really broke loose. My mother broke down. "I'm so glad you're *alive*," she said over and over again, tears flowing. "That's the only important thing. You're alive!"

"I'm glad to see you, Don," Dad said. "Really, I am." I could see tears in his eyes, too. His tone showed me how he was suffering, how bitterly disappointed he was, though genuinely glad I was at least alive.

It was a tremendous strain on all of us.

I couldn't blame them. No man of twenty-six should have to be faced with parents weeping because their son is a thief. I finally had my identity, all right. A real great image! My betrayal of my parents was a physical pain.

I spent a few days drying out from speed and alcohol, and, as time went on, the tension eased and we could talk without everyone breaking down and crying.

Days passed and I heard nothing from the police, I began to wonder if the D.A. had decided not to prosecute, after all. But after a week, the investigating officer telephoned. "Don," he said in an ominous voice. "I've got bad news. The D.A. has decided to prosecute. You're under arrest. If you'll come on down, I'll have a bondsman waiting; you can post bail and get right out."

Arrested by telephone!

It was two or three months before everything was over and I was tried, convicted, and sentenced. I could have gotten as much as ten years. I could have been sentenced to San Quentin. Instead, I ended up with a five-year suspended sentence and seven months in the county jail.

I was to be domiciled at the Lincoln Heights Jail, known as the cockroach haven of the West Coast. I was officially booked in. It took twelve hours. I was searched, fingerprinted, mugged, assigned to a cell block, my clothes taken, new clothes issued. I had to wait for hours in line at each "station," listening to all the prison talk.

The prison officials and guards didn't say much. They had seen and heard it all. They just did their job, hardly aware they dealt with humans. You were just fingers to be fingerprinted. "Okay, roll your thumb"; faces to be mugged, "Hold it!"; bodies to be hung with drab clothes that made you look like the rest of several hundred blue shadows in the dingy darkness of the inner jail.

It really hit me hard when I was led to the cell block. I had always dreaded being closed in, locked up. The only time I'd ever had any real peace of mind was when I was free to move—to run. As soon as I found myself in a little steel cage and knew I couldn't go anywhere, I started trembling. The click of the lock sent shivers down my spine. Only then did the full force of what I'd done to myself hit me. I was a caged beast. I was in *jail*.

The capacity of the cell-block where I was assigned was thirty. The actual number of men housed was 100. We could take a shower only once a week, if that. If you wanted clothes washed oftener than the infrequent laundry collections, you had to wash them out in the commode.

There was a sink in each cell to wash your face and brush your teeth. If you could afford a tooth brush.

You could read a newspaper, magazine, or book if someone from outside supplied you, but when the reading material finally got to you, it was outdated, worn-out, and full of missing pages, like the lives of the inmates who couldn't remember half of what had happened to them in their chaotic existences.

There was plenty of pornography, but you had to pay

someone or do him a favor to get a look at his better class of illustrated reading.

There were set patterns for every trivial activity you wanted to engage in—a regular hierarchy of command among the prisoners—and I had to learn fast. To keep your money safe from skillful fingers, you had to put it in a Bull Durham sack and tie it to your shorts. To do almost anything, you had to go *through* someone.

On the outside, I had met a lot of different kinds of people, many with hang-ups and habits in conflict with society's values. I'd known many heavy drinkers, even alcoholics, who somehow managed to stay out of trouble. I had known men who liked good times, fast bikes, and loose women. This was the kind of crowd that attracted me. But, on the outside, there was a subtle difference between them and me.

In jail, however, I found I was locked up with 100 other guys just like me. A hundred men playing roles. It was eerie! I recognized these guys! As though I were in a house of mirrors, I saw myself fractured into 100 diffferent weird distortions of the same basic face.

All they were doing was competing to see who could tell the biggest lies. Whoever had the most far-fetched, interesting, and ridiculous story was the winner. They told each other lies and pretended to believe each other's lies. We all had the same problem: we didn't know who we were.

We were imposters, just as we had been on the outside, psychological freaks—men with some basic characteristic that was wrong, different, abnormal. And we were all trying to make up for it.

The first day I was there, a black Muslim, about my size, gave me a hard stare. His eyes were narrow slits and the feeling he projected was cold. Suddenly, without saying anything, he dropped to the floor and did 75 quick push-ups. He was telling me something. He was telling me he was a tough guy. He was warning me to respect his superiority.

Another strong man in the jail was a Mexican named Pedro. He was only five-feet, two-inches tall. But he bragged about how he'd make himself strong by lifting weights, and he did everything he could to provoke anyone he thought he could beat up, all to prove that, just because he was short, didn't mean he couldn't clobber you.

In spite of dissipation, I was big and brawny enough to keep a guy guessing as to my fighting ability—and courage. I kept my mouth shut while I surveyed the scene, and this helped me stay out of trouble.

But one man was curious. He was a short, balding man with rimless glasses and a pinched face, as though he'd been an accountant and had ruined his eyes poring over books for forty years. "Musgraves," he said one day while we were getting our daily exercise in the cell block's long corridor, "I heard from the grapevine you souped a safe and got off with ten thousand dollars. Had a big holiday in Honolulu."

I snickered.

"That's all right. You're smart not to spell it out. That's why I've had my eye on you. After I serve this stretch, I'm going to set up a real organization. I'm going to compete with the Mafia. I had the whole thing set up when some rat informed on me. Anyway, you and I could really swing it, because we've got brains. Not like the rest of these idiots."

The same old, tired story, whether from the mouth of an illiterate pimp from downtown L.A. or an artist busted on possession. Most of them had one trait that had made them vulnerable.

I was getting stir crazy when the news was passed around that a group of us, including me, would be sent out into the mountains to train as fire fighters.

After two weeks I found myself attending a four-week training program in the use of trucks, hoses, shovels, and pickaxes. This was really great. I was out in the open air. I would be doing something worthwhile—something that took guts and led to heroic acts; something that would be difficult only when and if a major conflagration flared up in the trees and brush. Or, so I thought.

I was still with jailbirds. The black Muslim was one of the group. So was Pedro, and a dozen others.

I was quickly disillusioned about the glamour of the job. Wielding a heavy pickax was to be the *major* pastime once we finished "school."

Still, it beat the cell. We were out in God's country,

where we could get fresh air, sunshine, exercise, and a feeling of *space*! Where we could almost forget we were prisoners.

During the latter part of our training, I returned from a hot summer's day of field instruction and had just stepped out of the shower, a towel around me, when I skidded to a stop on the wet concrete floor.

I saw the back of someone who had to be a woman! "What's going on here?" I asked myself. I had to be dreaming. A woman? In the Fire-fighting School?

Adroitly, I managed a quick look in passing. It *was* a guy, all right. But he had all the curves in the right places.

I forgot about "her" and, in a few days, we had finished our course and were trucked to the Wayside Honor Camp in a remote part of the Angelus Mountains north of Los Angeles. The structures included four barracks sleeping twenty-five men each, a mess hall, equipment garages, and sheds and officers' quarters.

Six Los Angeles County deputy sheriffs were our "fathers," and the Los Angeles County Fire Department supervised our work.

A few days after we'd gotten accustomed to the routine, I was heaving the huge pickax over my shoulder when someone said, "Professor?"

It was the black Muslim, Pete Burroughs.

"How long you in for?" I asked.

Burroughs cocked his head. "I think the judge say about a year."

"Why are you a black Muslim, anyway?"

He scratched his beard. "Why are *you* nowhere? How I know why, man? It just something to be in, I guess. I mean, you got to be something, okay? Maybe *you* lucky and has a family. Old man an' lady. All that jazz. Me?" He spat. "No one. My old lady too busy buzzin' aroun' the bars to mind me. I don' know who she live with about the time I come along, so maybe even *your* old man could be my father for all I knows. But, when you in the organization, you got someone. They's yore brother and sister, papa and mammy. They looks after you."

"You know, Burroughs," I said, "I never quite understood this Muslim stuff. Just what do you guys believe, anyway?"

He gave me a cool, vacant look. "I don't get you. I mean, I don't exactly know, see? I mean, I never pay much attention to all the different things we suppose to think. I mean about politics and all that jazz. But, they teach you you okay like everyone else. You big guy and you can lick *them*. I was chicken before I join Muslim. Now, I real tough guy and anyone bother me, I fix them."

"What kind of work were you doing on the outside?"

"I work in a warehouse but they make big deal out of it, jus' forget couple little things, they can me. You know. Just cuz I black."

As I lay in my bunk later, trying to sleep, my muscles still twitching from the unaccustomed physical labor, I thought about the Muslim.

He wasn't such a bad guy, just had some screwy impressions about life. And I began to see we both had accused others of keeping us down. Some of Burrough's problems were different from mine. Yet, we were both here. We both had hang-ups, and we'd both ended up in the same place.

A few days later, I learned more about the man who I had thought was a woman. His name was Chet Wakefield. The bulls had given him the job of staking out the lines and tallying progress. Easy paper and pencil stuff.

I'd noticed some of the inmates ribbing him, but it wasn't until I came close up one time that I got the picture. He was a very effeminate man but wasn't willing to accept the role some of the guys assigned to him.

Pedro was especially abusive to him. "Why you no come to my bunk tonight, punk?" I heard him say.

When Wakefield shook his head and tried to move away, Pedro pushed him so he fell over a pick.

Later, I talked with Chet. He was really unhappy. "I can't help being this way," he said. "And some of this is my fault. Sometimes, I feel so strongly drawn towards some of these fellows, I kind of play up to them, I guess. I have this darn impulse. Conflicts. But then they want to push it too far."

"Why don't you try really developing your muscles?"
I suggested. "They could put you on the line if you did
some working out. If you could kind of beef up your
physique, maybe the men wouldn't be so attracted to
you."

Chet sighed. "I don't know if I could do that or not."

Whenever I was around Red, I was a different man.
Red and I hit it off because we both thought we were
swingers.

We played games with each other, acting out skits,
inventing whole dialogues. "That's a groovy floor show,"
Red would say, pointing to the clouds in the sky as we
gouged away at the rock at our feet. "See that broad
with the fluffy skirt?"

"Listen, Red," I said one day, pointing across the
canyon. "I'll bet you and I can ride this bike right down
that hill and up the other side faster than you could throw
a rock across it." I mounted the pick handle and stomped
on the ground with my foot as though I were starting
a motorcycle.

One fellow, though, one-upped us both. He was a
skinny thirty-year-old man of German descent whose father had been born and raised in the "old country."
Phil had picked up the heavy gutteral accent and a lot
of German words. He didn't need a partner to put on
his dramas. From listening to his father and his friends
at the German club, and watching phony TV programs,
he could take all the parts himself.

His favorite setting was a Nazi concentration camp.
Sometimes he'd be the German officer talking to another
officer; other times, he'd take the part of a guard con-
versing with a Jewish prisoner. Sometimes he played the
role of a German trying to sell skins.

It was sick, grisly, but for the kind of audience he
had, it was irresistible. When he got turned on, he broke
us up so much we could hardly work.

Out of a period of ten years, he hadn't been out of
jail for as much as one entire year at a time. Usually,

he'd be back in after only a few weeks on the outside. He never did anything serious enough to get sent to San Quentin or some other state institution.

He was addicted to prison. He was also addicted to pills, a speed freak. As soon as he'd hit the streets, he would find a connection. He'd consume as many as 200 pills a day.

Other men had other problems. Two bragged that they were karate experts. But I'd seen enough karate in the Service and on TV to know they were lying.

I don't think I saw one man there who wasn't playing a role.

During the early part of my sentence, I had insisted Loris get a divorce.

Loris didn't want a divorce. She and her family didn't believe in it. "I still love you, Don," she said when she came to the camp to visit me. She'd brought Mike and Lynne, and that was worse, because it made me feel all the more guilty and unworthy. Of course, Mike was only three and a half years old. Loris told him that I was working here and it was too far to come home every day.

I had told her I wasn't even sure what love meant. I certainly had not shown I knew the meaning of love, or why would I have treated her the way I had?

She finally agreed to file for divorce.

Meanwhile, I had written Jo Ann, the cocktail waitress in San Francisco. She was my kind. Maybe with her, I could hack it.

I knew who I was, at last. I was like Red and the other "happy" people who were tearing down mountains to help Smoky Bear keep California green.

But it was Red who suddenly jolted me out of this kind of thinking.

One evening he stopped by the barracks where I had my bed. "Well, Don Juan, what're you up to this Saturday night?"

Thinking he was starting one of his usual dramatic

skits, I replied, "I thought I'd drop up to 'Frisco and see Jo Ann. Why don't you pick up some chick and we'll double date? We can have a real blast."

"No, I mean it. You busy?" Red was serious.

"Actually, I was just going to read."

"Wondered if you wanted to come to the AA meeting with me?"

I laughed. "*You?*"

"Listen, Don, I got a girl friend on the outside. If she's still waiting for me, it would be worth it. She's almost as goodlooking as your wife. You know, Musgraves, something's been bothering me for a long time —puzzling me."

"Yeah? What's that?"

"You know, Musgraves—you just got to be nuts. To do the things you do and have a babe like that. Wow!"

"That's what the fuzz say," I answered. "What are you doing, anyway, going establishment on me?"

"No. I just want to get that monkey off my back. If Julie's still waiting for me on the outside, I might have a chance."

"But—the AA? *Here?*"

"Sure. It's part of their program. They're supposed to be rehabilitating us. Remember? What have you got to lose?"

People at the AA meeting did tell a lot of interesting yarns. I didn't let Red know, but I zeroed in on everything they said—and believed them. I identified with every detail, every word, every emotion. These people were just like me—except they had quit drinking.

They had come from nearby communities to get together in jail so any interested inmate could join in. That really generated a good feeling, too. And they had found something to help them stay off the bottle.

For my part, I knew that, like Phil and his pills, as soon as I hit free country, I'd be back sucking on the bottle. Not these guys. They had kicked it. How?

They talked about some books, and one man said he'd bring me one at the next meeting.

They'd kindled something. I ended up really hooked. At the next meeting, the guy wasn't there. Then, a few days later—I could hardly believe it, it was such a coincidence ... or was it?—I found that book in a trash can near the barracks, as though someone had planted it there just for me. It was entitled, *The Twelve Steps of Alcoholics Anonymous.*

I studied it, from cover to cover; then all over again. Part of it was written in layman's language about a relationship with God. I skimmed that, concentrating on the actual mechanics of how to get along without drinking.

One of the steps was admitting you are an alcoholic. By now I was ready to go that route. I was finally able to face myself and admit it.

Another step was finding someone to whom you would be willing to "confess" your shortcomings, lapses, and past life. In James 5 it says, "Confess your faults, one to another, and pray that you may be healed." I decided to take a raincheck on that one. There was no one at the Wayside Honor Camp I wanted to confess to—not even Red.

But the part about praying ... I began to try that one. I also wrote some letters, as the steps suggested, to people whom I'd wronged, telling them I was sorry.

I began to feel better right away. I experienced a new kind of expectancy about life.

It was winter now, and I lay awake in the barracks listening to the wind blowing, meditating on those twelve steps. I thought about the praying, and I started getting a warm feeling—a glowing, tingly feeling. I fell asleep praying, still feeling that way.

The next day, I wrote to Jo Ann and told her to forget me. I told her I knew what my problem was, now, and knew I could solve it, and had decided my efforts would be to put my family back together again.

Then, I wrote Loris! I told her to forget it, too—forget the divorce.

I begged her to visit me again.

In the letter, I told her I had found the answer to my problem, there was hope for us, after all. The drinking problem could be licked.

115

I waited apprehensively for her reply.

Then I got a letter. She said she'd think about it.

When one Sunday she showed up, and smiling at that, I was so revved up it took an hour for me to calm down so we could really talk.

Chapter 11

"How does it look to you, Loris?"

"I just love the master bedroom. I've always wanted a private bath. Why, it's even got a dressing room . . . a *dressing* room!" Her voice rose in excitement. The children's "oooh's!" and "aaaah's!" added to the enthusiasm.

I had been successful in staying off the bottle for about seven months. I had been successful at work, too; in fact, we were now celebrating my promotion to manager by picking out a house to buy.

AA had done wonders. Musgraves had done wonders. We were a team, AA and I. During the balance of my prison term, I had worked hard at programming myself to a life without liquor. I'd done as suggested in the *Twelve Steps of Alcoholics Anonymous*: admitted I was powerless over alcohol and that my life had become unmanageable, made a fearless and searching inventory of myself, promptly admitted it when I went wrong, and tried to tell others about beating booze.

After my release, I had gone to live with my parents in Orange while Loris had continued living with her parents in a nearby town. We saw each other almost every day—she even attended AA meetings with me—and the idea was that she and I would live together again as soon as I reestablished myself.

When I was made Head Cook at Colony Kitchen, in Corona, Loris and I found an apartment in Orange— quite a distance from work but close to our families.

And now that I was the *manager* of the Kitchen, we

were optimistic enough to think that we could, at last, buy our own home, close to work!

For it seemed that the miracle had happened! I had been *free* for the longest period since high school—free from alcohol's possession of mind and body which had made a wreck of me and given me such a stinging taste of hell.

I had finally become a good husband and father, friends with my two children, Mike, now six, and Lynne, three. They were all inspecting the rambling master bedroom of this impossibly expensive three-bedroom, two-story house, snuggled in a new development of hundreds of homes clinging to gently sloping hills overlooking the freeway.

The thought of making a down payment, even under the GI Bill and the FHA, and of keeping up the monthly payments on a *house* staggered me.

Even the manager's pay at Colony Kitchen, considering the subtraction for my restitution payments, would not be enough to make haste this hastily unless I really watched the budget.

As we drove on to a more reasonably priced house, I clenched my teeth. Tears blurred the road. If only I hadn't lost all those years swigging on that stinking bottle, we *could* have afforded the two-story dreamhouse we'd just drooled over.

I worked like a house afire for the next few months. I established a new record for low food and labor costs. I drove myself relentlessly. In the few hours I could be home, I tried to make it up to Loris and the kids for all the overtime; of course, I was bushed.

Even to afford the house we finally started negotiations on, it was tempting to count on the money Loris brought in from her job. She was working as an assistant to a Santa Ana oral surgeon, a job she'd held ever since I'd taken off for Honolulu. I had told her she could quit any time, but I hadn't twisted her arm. I kept harping on how much it was going to cost buying a house, how much the furniture would cost.

"But we don't have to get a lot of expensive furniture all at once," Loris protested. "We can collect stuff as we go along."

"No way, baby You've had to do without too long already. We'll need a dishwasher and a dryer, especially, now that we've a new one on the way."

Loris had had morning sickness a few weeks ago. We'd shown our love for each other, and our confidence in the future, by planning for another baby—one that I could watch grow this time.

It gave me a tremendous shot of joyful anticipation.

But it had also prodded me to dig in at work and make enough money to do it all in style.

On the other hand, with Loris pregnant, I began to feel guilty letting her work much longer. She was long-suffering. She'd gone through hell as much as I had—and I had put her through it. I finally served an ultimatum: "Quit work!"

Everyone depending entirely on the income I was earning scared me a little, and I buckled down even more on the job so that nothing could prevent them from giving me a substantial raise. Up to now I had experienced no desire to drink.

I got to know Bruce Demos, the General Manager of the whole chain of Colony Kitchens. He was one of the most dynamic men I have ever known. He never rested.

Then one day I was stunned. He offered me a chance to try for the position of manager of *seven* stores!

He talked to me as if I were an equal partner.

The remarkable fact was, he trusted me. He knew about my conviction for robbing the safe at Nationwide Food Services, though neither he nor anyone else knew about those worthless checks I'd written in Hawaii or the liquor store stick-ups.

He knew I'd served time in the county jail.

I'd had to tell him all this when I was offered the job of manager.

"Man! Seven stores bring in around one hundred grand!" I exclaimed. "I can't believe you'd stick your neck out that far."

Demos hesitated a moment. "Musgraves, you've got a magic touch in restaurant management. Ordinarily, I'm not a gambler. But I think you got what it takes to make it!"

What he was proposing was so exciting, my mind was already constructing gleaming castles in the clouds, a lavish estate with lush gardens.

"There are a couple of things," he resumed. "Remember, I'm not promising you the *job*. I'm promising you the *chance* to show you can handle it. You've got three months."

"I realize that, Mr. Demos," I said. "But I can still taste it." Actually, I was so sure I'd make the grade, and so determined to, I felt as though I'd already done it.

"It's going to be real rough, Don," he warned. "I'm going to work your head off. Think of everything involved in managing just one store, like you're doing now. Then multiply that by seven. Then double *that*, Don, because, in order to make really sure you are the right man for the job, I'm going to make it even harder."

It turned out to be rugged, all right. He really put me through the mill. It was worse than working full time and taking full-time classes at Oklahoma State University. Manning's had been a picnic compared to this.

In six weeks, I was so spread out I was about to blow apart at the seams.

In the past, when I had had extreme pressure like this, whiskey was the only relief.

The AA meetings were doing me less good. I'd miss some of the meetings. When I did go, I couldn't concentrate, my mind was full of menus, money, and manpower. Feeling guilty about this, I once took a few minutes to write some letters to people telling them how sober I'd been since they had known me. One of the twelve steps was "confession," and one of those to whom I wrote was Joe Blair, at Oklahoma State University, a man for whom I had worked while attending classes.

I told him about my troubles and how I was progressing. This made me feel better but didn't diminish the pressures.

I was restless one Saturday evening when I'd come home for a rare short weekend and a home-cooked meal. After dinner, while Loris was reading the children a Bible story, I interrupted her: "Loris, honey. I'm going to the AA meeting. Then, maybe I'll go check on the store."

I had a strange sensation, as though someone were

calling me. As though I weren't in complete control. One part of me wanted to run to Loris and hold on to her, use her as an anchor against . . . whatever it was.

I was just as restless at the AA meeting. A wall was around me, shutting out what everyone was saying. I was only dimly aware of people talking to me and mumbled back foolishly. Dick Hammon, my "sponsor," to whom I'd confessed quite a lot of things that even Loris didn't know, seemed concerned, but I turned him off. "Forget it," I murmured. "I'm okay."

I almost staggered out. When I got into my car, it seemed to take off in a direction all its own. I had to exert considerable will to swerve into the parking lot of a market. I turned off the motor and sat in the car, trembling all over.

I could visualize the cash registers in the Colony Kitchen, the money bags, the *safe*. . . . In the registers there'd be around $1,000 and, in the safe, $4,000.

On my tongue, in my throat, burning its way down my esophagus, I could feel and taste something I hadn't even smelled for nearly a year and a half—whiskey. All of a sudden, I had a wild, consuming thirst.

If I were to have just one drink—just *one*—those eighteen months would go down the tubes. Such is the fate of the alcoholic.

And, if I *were* to have that one drink, and be back on that vicious merry-go-round, all I had worked for so long and so diligently would go up in smoke.

Smoke! I could smell it—an acrid tingling smoke, as though alcohol were burning.

What the . . . why don't you just rip off that dough and split?

My heart jumped. Ice crackled on my skull, down the back of my neck, my spine, into my legs. It was an actual voice roaring in the hollow of my brain.

Images of Loris, sweetly smiling—the lines of worry and suffering almost melted away after these idyllic months—and of the kids: little dynamo Mike, and stumbling, awkward Lynne.

I must be losing my marbles!

You have lost your marbles! The voice was so sharp this time it almost split my skull.

Yeah. You lost your marbles, all right, to pass up

a chance like this. It's a perfect set-up and the timing couldn't be better. Rip it off, sucker.

No! But something had hold and wouldn't let go, as if my arm were pinned behind my back.

I tried to pray. Already, I'd forgotten how.

As soon as things had started going right again, the prayers, the thoughts of God, had subsided like an ebb tide.

Desperately I tried to remember some of the words about God in the *Twelve Steps of Alcoholics Anonymous*, but I'd glossed over the spiritual parts—the parts about God. Now when I needed words and concepts, they wouldn't come. A hot, horny hand clamped my mouth shut, a hot wind, beaten by *wings* I could almost feel, burned my face.

The only words I could groan out were, "Okay . . . you win, stop tormenting me."

And I did. I drove directly to the Colony Kitchen in Corona where I had my office. I went to the girls at the cash registers and asked them for the night's take. It was a common practice to collect this periodically and put it in the safe in my office. We didn't like to keep too much in the registers.

There was a total of $1,000 in the registers, just as something had told me there would be.

I went to the safe where the money from forty-eight hours of brisk business had accumulated. Smoothly, as if my actions were being guided by the most expert pro, I collected the money, making a quick estimate as I put the bills in my attache case. There was more than $4,000 there, just as I knew there would be.

All this time I had a sickness in my gut, as though something still sane inside me was holding on for dear life, but was powerless to stop me.

From there I went straight to a bar, ordered Canadian Club and Seven-Up, and for three hours sat there staring at the glass.

I was breathing heavily, everyone was looking at me. One last-ditch line of defense must have been holding out but, in the end, I suddenly lifted the glass and drank the contents chug-a-lug.

A low, moaning sigh went up. I rose, turned around, and split.

Seven hours later, with just the clothes on my back and that attache case, I was on a plane for New Orleans.

The details of what happened next, the ups and downs of the *next* eighteen months, would be just another story I would have to tell. The pattern was the same—periods when I lived it up and at the same time was consumed to almost nothing—a mere shadow—by booze.

I returned and, in lieu of a jail term, was given the chance to pay back the more than $3,000 I had spent. For a while, I went back to Loris, and worked for the same boss as a relief cook, working for him so he could get back some of the money at the rate of $100 a month.

I'd work for a while, quit; go back to work, then go on another binge. For one month I stayed with my brother Dean on Catalina Island.

While he worked on a construction job, I'd lay on the beach drying out from our evenings sitting with a gallon jug of Red Mountain Wine.

We were alike: both alcoholics. Dean could hack work better. We were so much alike we got bored with each other's company, and I went back to the mainland and to AA for a while.

Some time during this roller coaster race through a dark tunnel of hell, Loris filed for divorce and got a judgment for child support. Our third child, Tracy, had arrived.

I got a job at a new restaurant in Orange County. For a while I was on the wagon, but I'd shoot pool with two of my co-workers—wild guys named Ken and Jim.

I was tempted by a glass of beer, hooked again, and the three of us took off to work at Lake Tahoe.

I might have just fizzled out—died of sclerosis of the liver somewhere between here and nowhere. That would have been the end of the story, except that before leaving Orange County, I wrote several hundred dollars worth of worthless checks.

Because of that, the story took another turn.

Chapter 12

The three of us, Ken, Jim and I, arrived weary and almost numb from the sudden change in temperature.

"Man, let's find us a pad to sack out in before job hunting," Ken suggested.

"No, you've got it wrong," Jim said. "We'll have to have a job. Otherwise they'll charge us the Lake Tahoe tourist rates."

"While you two figure out what to do, let's grab us some coffee," I said, spotting some cute chicks walking out of a cafe across the road. We went over and found stools.

"I've got a lead on Harrah's Club," Jim said. "My cousin worked here once and he said either club, Nevada or California, was a good outfit to work for, but you got to be fast."

"Right now, I don't feel so speedy." Ken yawned and stretched. The altitude got to all of us. "Hey, what did you guys do with the bennies?"

Jim reached in his pocket and pulled out a supply for all of us. By the time we had two more cups of coffee and a few of those pills, we set out to look for jobs. Harrah's Club, on the Nevada side, was the closest, so we sauntered in and applied. The application form's first question: "Do you have a criminal record?"

Not letting that stop me, I made up a whole new life.

The boss at Harrah's Club gave all three of us an interview together and hired us on the spot. Jim and I were to stay in the Nevada Club and Ken was to go across the street and do the evening shift. Because of all my *experience*, I was put on the morning shift.

Apartment hunting wasn't as easy. Many of the managers were skeptical about renting to three guys, but we finally located one manager who would rent to us as soon as we verified we had jobs at Harrah's. We brought our stuff in and crashed.

Soon after we reported for work, we discovered we were just three of a thousand employees hired each summer to cater to the tourists. There *was* plenty of overtime, since none of the clubs wanted to shut down. Each shift boasted three cooks, going full speed. I didn't let on, of course, that I could have shown them how to run a tighter kitchen.

I was happy to be just a flunky, working, partying, and gambling—losing myself. The hours were long and the pace was hectic, but only because we wanted it that way. Jim, Ken, and I were evenly matched. We couldn't get enough. None of us wanted to sleep like regular people did, so we had to rely on the extra bennies to get us through our shifts and then on to the parties.

This was our routine for the next few weeks. With overtime, I was able to draw about $1,000 per month. I even opened a savings account.

One morning while I was shoving hashbrowns and eggs around on the grill, the boss came up behind me and whispered, "I want to talk to you."

I looked around to see if anyone else was listening, then went on turning eggs and hashbrowns, my heart down to my Florsheims.

"Listen," he went on. "You've done a good job for us, Musgraves. But I'm risking losing my job. I'm not supposed to tell you this." I had to strain to hear him above the noise of the grill. "The Nevada State Police are going to pick you up when you finish your shift. As far as you're concerned, I didn't tell you. Okay?" He turned and walked off.

"Not now, Musgraves, not this way," I kept saying to myself. I knew it was a state law in Nevada that if you falsified a job application, there was a fifty-dollar fine and you could spend thirty days in jail. It was about time they had checked my application. That was what they wanted to see me about. I also knew once in that police station, they might decide to do some *more* checking—the kind that always turned up a SOLD OUT for Musgraves.

I worked that hour, which seemed more like four, until a lull hit. "Hey, Sam, take over for me for a few minutes, will you?" I asked the guy next to me. "I've got to go see John."

I headed down the back stairs, saw John, and then kept right on going, up and out through the casino just as the State Troopers were coming in the front with the boss, heading for the kitchen.

The apartment wasn't far away. I dashed in, picked up the .38 revolver Jim used for target practice and a couple of shirts, and went to a bar. I spent the next eight hours getting smashed.

Later that night, bombed out of my mind, I rapped on the door of the apartment. Jim pulled me in, making signs to be quiet.

"We have a message for you." Ken grinned. "The cop said, 'Tell him if he stays in California, we can't touch him.'"

I was too bombed to figure that one out.

"That's easy, Don," Ken said. "I hear Heidi's Pancake House needs someone. All you have to do is walk across the street and you're out of this state."

Ken was right. They did need someone at Heidi's. The job turned out to be even better than Harrah's, except for one of the other cooks on my shift. He was so revved up on bennies, when he went to flip pancakes, all he had to do was hold the pan—they flipped themselves.

There were all kinds of characters around like him. We kept up a steady stream of speed, alcohol, sex, wild parties, gambling, lying, and stealing our ways out to nowhere.

The season hit its peak and so did I. The money I had put in the savings account, over $700, was soon gone on drink, drink, and more drink. Then the gambling got to me. Because we had to keep working, we upped our quotas of bennies, and it wasn't long before I lost my judgment at the blackjack tables. I really thought someone was coming up behind me, looking at my cards. Every time I'd get into my car, I'd check the back seat to make sure no one was there.

I knew it would take a while for the FBI to check out my form in Washington, D.C. But, just the same, before reporting for work each morning, I'd drive around the place once or twice to make sure no State Troopers were waiting. As I cooked, I looked over my shoulder constantly. No one dared come up behind me too quietly or they'd have been flattened.

One morning while cleaning the stainless steel around the stove, I saw myself in it—a distorted jigsaw puzzle that had been jarred by someone and not quite righted. "I've got to get out of here," I thought. "Maybe they could use me back at the U." I was grasping at straws this time, making one last try. "My old friend Joe—surely he'll have something.

I got on the phone.

"Man, since I received your letter some months ago," he responded, "I've been trying to locate you. No one knows where you are. Yes, I have a job. Have you still got your head on straight?"

"Yes," I lied. "But things are a little slow here now." We talked some more and he told me about the job— a manager, again. I had convinced him that I could handle a manager's job!

It was a cold and lonely trip. I was poor company, shaky and sick often. Maybe I won't get this last chance, I thought. Maybe I'll just die along the road and be frozen stiff before they find my body . . . won't even know who I am. This wasn't the way I had planned to return to Stillwater again.

Joe was full of apologies when I arrived. "I'm really sorry, Don. But I couldn't convince the board you could handle the job." He looked at me with keen eyes. "Last year someone ripped off about $5,000. The board didn't feel they could take another chance. There's a place out on the highway that needs a manager."

I decided to take them on. Where could I go now, anyway? At least I would be busy, maybe a chance to pull myself back together.

I worked day and night and built up the owner's confidence in me. But, I kept on drinking. I'd go from bar to bar, looking for excitement. There wasn't any, not even any girls to pick up.

After working one month, I woke up on a Sunday morning knowing I had to leave. I couldn't hack it. I was going out of my skull.

Without much thought at all, I went to the restaurant, emptied the cash register as I always did to make a deposit, put the money in the safe—except for the $200 I deposited in my attache case.

Then I headed for the nearest car rental agency. My old Pontiac was leaking oil. I didn't think it would last any distance. I used my regular identification; the rental car was mine for two days.

I drove back to the motel, which was part of the business, and proceeded to take the license plates off my old car. I was going to put them on the rental car after I got out of town.

It was just three weeks before Christmas. When I arrived, only a fourth of the staff at the clubs was working. There were no jobs for me. I couldn't even get on shoveling snow.

I talked Jim into going to San Francisco so I'd have company. I didn't like being alone this time of the year. Jim must have felt the same way; he was willing to go along with a cheap room in a rundown hotel just so we could stay together. We both found jobs right away. I had $20 left.

The job was in a twenty-four-hour hamburger specialty place. You could order any kind of hamburger you could think up. The chef also had to be bouncer because of motorcycle gangs frequenting the area. I got double pay for the 6 p.m. to 2 a.m. shift, cooking. At 2 a.m. I put on a suit and tie and "directed traffic" out in front. I was supposed to keep people from ripping up the property or taking off without paying. The truth was, I was in such bad shape, anyone could have demolished me with a flyswatter.

After I'd worked two weeks, I got an advance. I was so sick the next day, I decided I'd had enough. I took off with the advance. With $200 in my pocket again, I decided to go south to Orange County. Christmas depressed me. I was as low as I'd ever been.

I pulled a favorite trick of mine, calling a motel and making reservations for a friend, Don Musgraves, who was flying in from Chicago. This set the stage for staying a week without paying.

I hadn't written to any of my family. For all they knew, I could have been dead. I was close enough to it—a walking skeleton. While driving, there were times I couldn't even remember where I had been. "Did I stop at that last stop sign?" I didn't know.

After I arrived in Orange County and had a few drinks, I called an old girl friend, who had since married. She and her husband invited me over to have dinner with them. It was Christmas Eve.

"Good to see you, Don." Georgia greeted me with a kiss under the mistletoe. We sat for an hour or so making small talk, then finally she blurted out, "Don, there's something we have to tell you."

"Yeah, what?"

"Your brother Dean is dead."

I was silent for a minute! "Yeah, yeah," I thought. "Probably from too much boozing and. . . ." Aloud, I said, "How did it happen?" I couldn't *feel* anything. I guess I knew it would happen someday.

A cerebral hemorrhage, they told me.

"Where were *you*?" Georgia asked.

"Nowhere," I said. "Nowhere." I got up and walked out the door. "Oh, God!" I asked myself, "what is wrong with me? Why don't I *feel* anything?"

Chapter 13

Twenty of them were shuffling down the sidewalk as the morning downtown traffic buzzed by, twenty assorted shapes and sizes, a few black, all in the same faded blue cotton shirts and levis, clanking down the street in close formation, held together at the waists by chains, wrists manacled. Across shirt backs and down pant legs, in large, bold orange letters were the words: ORANGE COUNTY JAIL.

Accompanying them were olive-uniformed men with pistol belts, two of them in the lead, two a few paces behind.

Marching two-by-two, the column was directed to the extreme right when pedestrians scurried by—pedestrians who rushed on for some distance before turning to *stare*; women pulling little children who craned their necks, looking back wide-eyed.

Some prisoners hung their heads, others sneered.

Up marble steps, they clomped, then into the corridor, echoing the sound of their feet, the noise of their chains.

For weeks after my arraignment, I couldn't get this picture out of my mind, or the *feeling* of being herded along the streets of Santa Ana, the county seat, *branded*. People looking at us, thinking, "Prisoners! Keep your distance. They might break loose. Explode. Bite."

As individuals, we were nothing. Yet almost everyone in the group had ended up in it because he'd tried to prove he *was* someone. Anyone. You name it.

And they'd ended up only as numbers. With free people staring.

130

The failure of rehabilitation begins with the shake-down, the stripping, and the exhibition in the streets and courts.

What irony that I had asked for this, not only in trampling on others' rights, but in giving myself up!

After learning that my brother Dean was dead, I'd gotten several jobs in Orange County, right under the noses of those looking for me. I'd manage to work out a shift, then get drunk for a couple of days, then go on to another restaurant and work a day. Then, not even able to work an entire shift and my pockets empty, my motel rent way overdue, I walked out with only the clothes on my back.

I walked to my mother's house. She wasn't home. I hadn't seen her or talked to her for many months. No one except Georgia knew I was back in Orange County.

I cooked myself the first meal I'd had in three days —eggs, bacon, toast, coffee. After finishing breakfast, I started to read the newspaper. My mind wandered. I flung the paper down. One more escapade had come to an end. I would give myself up one more time.

At that time, I didn't realize what low was, although I was really sick from booze—a complete physical wreck.

I was to be tried and sentenced separately for each of five counts: writing bad checks, non-support, violation of Los Angeles County probation for the North American heist, transporting a stolen vehicle across a state line, and defrauding an innkeeper (the motel manager I'd just walked out on).

There was enough paper on me, if I got all the toughest judges, to earn me sixty years!

Even the thought of serving sixty years didn't dig as sharply into my soul as the humiliation of that downtown stroll in the role of outcast.

Smarting under it, I groped out wildly for some comfort. I wrote a letter to Loris to let her know I was back in town—

Dear Loris,

I don't have any idea what your reaction to this letter will be. I don't suppose it really matters, but there are a few things I'd like to say. Some time ago, I got myself in trouble and false pride and a fantastic criticism of myself has kept me in trouble ever since.

Loris, I know I've put you through hell. Something no human being has a right to do to another. But even through this and after it's too late, I have to tell you I've always loved you and, more than that, I've always needed you terribly. Something I found almost impossible to admit. I don't know why, exactly. I don't suppose it matters now. My words must sound pretty empty. They're still the truth.

There are plenty of reasons why you should never even speak to me again. But I'd hate to think one of them was because I couldn't say what I really feel, and know to be the truth. Loris, I'll never give up trying to find a way for us to be a family. I might as well warn you. That is, unless you convince me you're happier the way it is. If you are, that's what I want, too. Either way, when I get out, I'll send you money for the children. I would appreciate your letting me write to them. I think I can communicate something just by having you read it to them. It may sound comical, but I really think I have something constructive to say to them now. I would appreciate being able to.

I get my just reward on January 27. I have no idea what the sentence will be.

If you decide you don't want to answer this letter, I won't blame you. And I won't bother you with any more from me. Just remember one thing: so far, I don't know of any rule that says two people in our circumstance have to stay this way forever. And no one has the right to make rules for another human being that say, "That's it. You're not allowed to try any more."

No. 46488
—Don

I have already reported Loris' answer. She ended

her letter with: "I wish there was something I could say that would make you feel like the heel you are, but then I guess you know better than anyone else who you are. I only hope that every day of your confinement is like an eternity and every night one long continuous nightmare."

It was actually a very real blessing that Loris encouraged me to write to our children—Mike, Lynne, and even Tracy, who was only about two years old. Loris sometimes let seven-year-old Mike write his own letters, and she wrote down what Lynne wanted to say. So, for the first time in well over a year, I was communicating with my children again, children who thought their daddy was "away working."

The letters I wrote to my children and the replies I received kept me from cracking up completely. Regardless of how much I deserved Loris' wrath, it still hurt. Her stinging words were caused by her own torments, I knew. She still loved me, yet felt she couldn't trust me to change—ever. Her family, with all the reason in the world, were pressuring her to keep her distance from me.

The scene around me added to my misery. I was crowded in with too many others like myself. The overall jail situation was really bad news. There were no planned activities. We were locked up almost the whole time in the cell complex, six men to a cell.

The only chance we had to stretch our legs was when individual cell doors were opened during the day to let us into the block's long hall for a few hours.

There was no library, no reading matter. Books, magazines, and newspapers were an individual responsibility. If you had friends or relatives who brought you things to read, great. If not, tough.

The only books anyone tried to give us were Bibles. There was a scattering of New Testaments in the complex, but few guys even opened them to look at the pictures. Of course, some of them were used to smuggle in dope.

The only outside space was a small courtyard in the center of the jail, with tiers of cell complexes on four sides.

Someone, some time in the distant past, had decided

the open courtyard would make a good handball court. The authorities scheduled time on the court. It worked out at sixty minutes once a week per prisoner.

The worst ordeal was being jammed in with so many mental freaks of one kind or another, without sufficient supervision to keep some of the stronger from preying on the weaker or to shield some of us from ourselves, our own violent emotions and aggressions, impulses we could not control in jail or out.

There were no jobs to do, nor any recreation to occupy us. All day long we played evil games with each other, threatened and beat each other. It was a jailbird jungle where the animals were pitted against each other.

One day we were standing in line inside the tank, in line for clean clothing, the once-weekly exchange at the laundry room.

For security reasons, we had to march briskly in straight lines and get the exchange over so that the next cell complex could take its turn.

But one man in our unit was on an emotional jag. Although he knew the rules, wanted clean clothes and knew full well he was no match for Sammy, our cell block's great dictator, he goofed off at the end of the line.

Sammy, whom the guards depended on to keep our unit disciplined, turned around, took in the scene, then stepped to the rear of the line, raised his sledge-hammer fist, and rammed it hard into the guy's face. He hit the floor like a sack of cement off a truck's tailgate.

Sammy's expression was something to see: his eyes constricted to a cat's narrow slits, hate sparking. I'd never seen a man's pupils constrict and stay that way for so long. There was a satanic force in those eyes that said Sammy was a killer.

Suddenly, it all became clear to me why these men were here, why we were all here, no matter how good or how lousy our backgrounds had been.

We weren't here because we came from broken homes, or because our parents were so wealthy that they'd spoiled us rotten. We weren't here because our schools were corrupted by Communism or our society too repressive.

These weren't the reasons we were loathsome creeps:

Sammy, a blood-thirsty tyrant; Rob, a burglarizing doper; Jake, a speed maniac with pills and hot cars on the freeway to hell; and I, an alcoholic and liquor store stick-up bum. These weren't the reasons we were all imposters, aping man but behaving like demon-possessed beasts.

Satan was the reason.

Now I knew why I had pulled all those crazy things—things that didn't make sense, things for which there was no visible explanation except to hurt someone.

But I had not consciously wanted to hurt anyone. That's why it had never made sense—until now.

It had been Satan all along.

He had sat with me in that plush office at Manning's and coaxed me into peeking into my boss' pay envelope, then into dipping into the till.

He had been my chauffeur during those wild drives in the blues of the night, steering me into go-go joints, cocktail bars, and honkytonks where the music was loud and the women loose.

Satan had dissuaded me from keeping that first appointment with Alcoholics Anonymous, had programmed me to become Don Cook, high-flying "Lawyer" and Hawaiian swinger, who got bombed out and wrote bad checks.

In Las Vegas he had toyed with me in that motel room as I toyed with the pistol he'd goaded me into buying. Then he'd carefully instructed me on how to pull armed robberies at liquor stores.

With glee, Satan had let me alone long enough to climb back up out of the black pit, on the ladder of AA, but kept from me the spiritual meaning behind the *Twelve Steps of Alcoholics Anonymous.*

He had allowed me to rise again, higher then ever! Then, just when I was on the brink of final success, in a parking lot at night he had physically wrestled with me. "Rip it off!" I could hear him now, as I plodded in line to the laundry room.

I recalled the sickness in my gut as I drove to Colony Kitchen and cleaned out its safe, a sickness that was a prelude to alcohol's ravages now that I was traveling at tangents again, to New Orleans, and all the other places on the wild bumpy ride of Hades' Ferris Wheel.

Satan is that evil genie in the bottle, ready to do your bidding—for a price.

Knowing Sammy was possessed by Satan and that I was likewise possessed, I knew, sooner or later, Sammy and I would have our own showdown.

The letters I was getting from my children seemed to be preparing me for something. They seemed to be pleading, without knowing it, for a change to take place, now that I had recognized the true source of my failures.

I received two letters from them near the end of the month. Mike's went:

> Dear Daddy,
> I always say your name in my prayers. I hope Mommy lets me play baseball this summer. I don't want to go to summer school. Lynne got sick and threw up. But she is all rite. Love Mike

This letter was a revelation! Loris had been having the children pray and go to church all this time.

She kept right on nourishing their love in me and belief in God and teaching them to pray!

After reading Mike's letter, I felt I was getting closer to some kind of inner explosion.

I looked up, tears flowing down my face, my mind in the clouds, and saw Sammy's wicked sneer, his eyes slits, piercing, marking me.

The other letter was from Lynne:

> Dear Daddy,
> I love you. I hope you'll be my valentine, Daddy. We went to Aaron's birthday party yesterday.
> I hope you'll be home soon to play with me. I have dishes for you to play house with me, but I'm not mad at you just because you've been at work so long, because I love you very much and I know you'll come back soon.
> Daddy, I got a haircut and I hope you like it when you get home.
> Lynne

I reread Lynne's letter several times. Something was odd about the letters from the children. They didn't go along with the words Loris had used, her opposition to us ever getting together again, her hopes I'd be locked up in the Orange County Jail until it crumbled in ruins.

But, if she had no intention of ever living with me again, why did the children write as though I would be home—and soon? Especially, "and soon." None of us knew, least of all Loris and I, how long a stretch I would be serving. It was almost as though they were prophesying. It really puzzled me.

I had gone back to court, meanwhile, to enter a plea on the nonsupport charge, which was an irony in itself, now that I'd developed at least some relationship with the children I'd neglected so long. I was chained up as before, along with more than a dozen other inmates, and escorted to court. A different judge presided. He seemed tough. I pleaded guilty and sentencing was set for two weeks from now.

With that bitter irony digging at me, as if Satan were taunting me, I started feeling sick and blue again.

The next day I picked up one of the New Testaments lying around. I read a few pages, shook my head. I couldn't make sense out of it.

The next day as I lay in my cell, alone because the other five who shared my suite were at court, I turned away from the dirty concrete wall and faced the bunk opposite. After a few moments, I realized I was staring at something relatively rare in the cell—a book. Jake, who had that bunk, wouldn't mind my looking at it. I reached over and picked it up. It was *The Cross and the Switchblade*, by Dave Wilkerson.

I thumbed through it. It kept mentioning the name, Jesus Christ. After reading several pages, I lost interest. Something seemed to be pushing it away from me and I threw it down.

The next day I noticed the same book in the same place, almost challenging me, it seemed.

I shrugged. I'd try again. Anything to get my mind off my troubles. Then I got hooked by it. I read it for the rest of the day.

After dinner I went right back to reading. I had never before heard anyone speak or share the kind of testimony in this book, expressing the idea that Jesus Christ was not only the Son of God, but had power over people's lives.

137

People had often said to me, "You ought to go to church," or "You ought to talk to my pastor." But the guys about whom this book was written were not church-goers, but drug addicts, alcoholics, pimps, prostitutes—people like me, who had seen life at its ugliest.

It seemed freakish that such people were saying, "Praise the Lord," falling to their knees, praying, asking for salvation.

During the next few days, as I kept thinking about it, I began to wonder if maybe there wasn't something to this person, Jesus Christ. I dug up the New Testament and really tried to read it. I spent hours—days—reading it. But it was written in the language of the King James Version, and it was hard for me to get with it, to make heads or tails of it.

Bitterly disappointed, I tucked it away, and the message of *The Cross and the Switchblade* along with it.

But . . . I couldn't tuck it away for long. There *was* an answer in the New Testament. There had to be. Otherwise, all those hoodlums in New York's ghettos wouldn't have been miraculously transformed from killers and creeps to witnesses who worked among their people to save souls.

I started reading the New Testament again, searching, searching, searching, until my eyes fell on I John 1:12, "For as many as receive him, to them gave he the power to be the sons of God."

I swallowed hard and re-read those brief words: the print leaped up to me, suddenly communicating in a way other than words.

Then, an explosion in my brain. A sudden white light *flooding* the darkness. I realized God was actually speaking to me, heard His voice saying, "Receive my Son."

I was jarred so hard I shook.

God had spoken to *me!*—"Receive my Son."

Great. But—how do you do that?

Well, I'd gone to one of the chapel services in the jail one Sunday and had happened to pick up a piece of paper and stuck it in my pocket. It was the *Sinner's Prayer*, put out by Billy Graham. I dug into my pockets:
"Dear Lord,

"I am a sinner. I confess that I have sinned. I confess

that I need your forgiveness. Will you forgive me and come into my heart and change me and make me what you want me to be? In the name of Jesus."

I felt so close to everything, now! I prayed, using these words. Nothing happened. I was close, all right—so close and yet so far! Just as "outside" was close, just beyond those bars—but oh so far.

I was hardly aware of time passing, as I read a few lines of the New Testament and repeated the prayer periodically, tears in my eyes, tears because I knew what kind of man I was and I was genuinely sorry.

I kept crying and saying the *Sinner's Prayer.*

When dinner came that night, I was still lying there, facing the wall, weeping. Weeping quietly and murmuring this prayer over and over and over. Finally, I stopped crying. But I couldn't get that prayer out of my mind.

All through the darkness of that night, I tossed and turned.

Daylight came. Then it was time again for soup, the same old watery soup, same old stale bread, same leers and foul epithets hurled just to prove the hurlers existed. Same old jail cell. Same old everything. Everything except . . . *me!*

Chapter 14

Suddenly, there was a new occupant in the Orange County Jail. His name was Jesus Christ. He was standing as close to me in my cell as you are to this book. His presence gave me the literal feeling that thirty years of degradation had been lifted from me.

I knew the weightless feeling space adventurers must have. I felt light enough to walk right through the bars.

I knew in an instant what freedom meant; though I was locked up on the third floor of that heap of concrete, I was a free man. Spiritually, *I could go anywhere* I wanted to go.

What ecstasy! I had no doubts I was a changed man! The cancer of sin had been cured! I felt like laughing and dancing, singing and praising the Lord!

How suddenly it had all broken through my despair and suffering! How suddenly Jesus seemed to appear there with me! I couldn't exactly see Him with my eyes, but my *mind*—my heart—saw Him clearly.

The inmates in the cell block were too intent on their own struggles to notice the startling change in me at first, but I was too full of new life to keep it to myself for long.

In the cell block, there was an inmate named Murray whom I had hated, a fat, sloppy, unkempt man—even for this environment—with every tooth in his head rotten. He had been arrested 180 times for drunk-in-public. He was out of touch with reality and he babbled incoherently and constantly.

Until today I had hated his guts because—*because he reminded me of what I myself was going to be like soon.*

140

Just before soup and bread, he was standing at the window of the cell complex, looking out, babbling. I strolled close. A cool, moist breeze was puffing in. Suddenly, not even realizing what I was doing, I put my hand on his shoulder and made him turn enough so that I could look him in the eye. Then, "You know what, man? *Jesus loves you!*"

I had felt my vocal chords move, my lips move. I had heard my own voice, deep with feeling, utter these words. *Yet, I hadn't the slightest foreknowledge I was going to say these words!*

We just looked at each other for a moment. I don't know which one of us was the more shocked. But I do know it frightened *him* exceedingly! He *ran!*

Murray kept his distance, but my love stood right beside him.

It was the strangest feeling I'd ever had—*loving* someone. Loving a repulsive drunk who smelled like he'd spent his life in garbage heaps.

If I could love someone like him, I could love anyone.

I could feel Jesus standing at my side, full of love for *me!* I laughed. "Thank you, Jesus," I said.

It dawned on me an hour later that I had done what thay call *witnessing*. I was conscious that Murray was the first man to whom I had witnessed since I had been saved. What a blessing! And—who needed it worse than Murray?

Maybe I couldn't change Murray—at least, not right away, not now. But God could change him. Perhaps my words would echo in his soul for a while.

I was so delirious with my new gift, I wasn't conscious of what was going on around me for a day or two or three.

I do know I was groping for a more accurate way to define and understand the change. I was aware of reading the Bible, searching for Scriptures to explain this phenomenon. I was not sure just what to call what had happened to me.

Then I ran across John 3:3: "Verily, verily, I say unto thee, Except a man be born again, he cannot see the kingdom of God."

I knew what had happened! I had been born again!

Everything was different. I was different. I looked at everything around me as if seeing for the first time. Ev-

141

erything had new meaning. Every little thought and act had to be re-examined in the light of this new being who was I. I had to become acquainted with a new being.

On the same day I realized I was born again, I had gone to the store where we were allowed to go twice a week to buy razor blades, soap, toothbrushes, cigarettes, and writing paper. Through sheer habit, I bought four or five packs of Pall Malls. When I was back in the cell, I lit up a smoke and took a deep breath . . . and almost choked!

I tossed over the Pall Malls. "Hey, Jake. Have some cigarettes. I don't need them any more. I've got Jesus."

It had happened again! Words I hadn't planned to say tumbling out of my mouth!

Jake's jaw popped open. "Man," he finally said, "you've flipped out! Guard! Guard!"

I jumped to my feet, putting a hand on his arm. "Cool it, Jake," I said. "Don't call the guard."

"What do you mean, man? You've gone psycho. I ain't taking any chances—"

"No, no. I'm okay. I'm okay," I said. "I just don't need them any more, that's all. There's nothing wrong with me. Nothing wrong with me at all."

Frowning, he studied my face, then shrugged. "Well, okay, Musgraves. But if you come after me, you'd better do it right the first time or you'll be, like dead."

I smiled. "Don't worry about that."

He went back to his bunk, mumbling, "I've got Jesus!' Cripes! And you say you ain't flipped!"

From the reaction of Murray and Jake, I began to wonder if I wasn't in for a rough time. I knew I was just too full of love and joy and God to be quiet about it. I also knew that the Bible said we should witness to our brethren. Oddly, though, the possibility that it would cause me a lot of trouble didn't seem to bother me much.

I just couldn't worry!

This was another aspect about myself I had to get used to—this absolute inner peace and security, serenity and self-assurance.

I'd just never had these qualities before. Now they were mine all at once, one hundred per cent, without my having really done anything to bring it about—except having read the Bible, thought, and prayed for about a week.

I knew what it was—miracles. God's miracles were working right now, in the twentieth century, just as they had during Jesus' lifetime and when He arose from the dead to instruct and inspire His apostles.

In a couple of days, I was to return to court for sentencing on the nonsupport charge. Just before Jesus had come into my life, I had started getting edgy. Several of the men in our cell complex had already been before this judge. None of them had received less than nine months.

Suddenly, it no longer worried me.

A day or two before I was to appear before the same judge, the prison chaplain, Pastor Jim Firth, came by our cell complex on his usual twice-weekly rounds. It was his habit to stop at each complex and holler in, "Anyone want to see the chaplain?"

Usually, he either drew a blank or a chorus of rude jokes. It seemed that several in our cell block were not only "neutral" on Christianity, but definitely anti-Christian. They would do their best to run down Christ, God, and Christianity.

At least one inmate was an avowed Satanist. As I told Loris later in a letter, "This place here bears no resemblance to the kindergarten I was in up in the Angelus Mountains. Some of the guys here would be great testimonials. Their lives are directed by the Princes of Satan's Kingdom. Not just ordinary devils, but deserving the rank of a Prince.

"These guys are not fooling. Many of them have dedicated their lives to destroying Christianity in order to justify their own existence."

Having lived among these men twenty-four hours a day, seven days a week for two months and having heard them spout blasphemies, I knew Chaplain Firth had no easy job. Now that I'd been born again, I winced all the more at obscenity thrown at him when he stopped, hoping to find someone who wanted to hear the Lord's Word, or to try to help someone.

I fully understand the conditions under which prison chaplains work. What denominations they represent and how they are employed doesn't matter. Theirs is a thankless task. They hold on because of the strength given them by Jesus Christ.

Before my conversion, I had gone once or twice to

Sunday services conducted by Chaplain Firth. I had found myself among a handful of others, staring around at the empty benches and wondering if the churches on the outside were as unpopular as those in the jails.

I now anticipated Chaplain Firth's visit and was ready to hop over to the door to talk with him when he came by with his rather weary, "Anyone want to talk with the chaplain today?"

"I do!" I shouted much more loudly than necessary when I heard his call. He looked in.

There was an awkward silence. I finally found my tongue. "Actually, Chaplain Firth, I don't have any problem. I, well, just wanted to tell you something. I—I became a Christian. A couple of days ago."

He smiled. "You know, I believe you. You look different. No kidding."

I grinned sheepishly. "I'm sure it shows, Chaplain. You know, these guys in here think I'm some kind of nut. Sometimes I think I am, too. I say the weirdest things lately."

"Those things sound weird," the chaplain said, "to people who aren't with Jesus yet. And to those who aren't, well, newly born, so to speak."

I shifted my weight from one foot to the other, hung onto the bars uneasily, as though to hold him another minute, two more minutes, although I knew he had many other cell blocks to visit.

"There is something bothering you, Musgraves, isn't there? I mean, are you sure you don't want to ask me something?"

I laughed. "It seems crazy, but I don't really know how to pray. I read most of the Bible this past week and the whole New Testament but—"

"Praying's no big thing, Don," the chaplain said. "Put it like this: think about how we're talking now. Well, you can talk to God the same way. Just like when you're talking to a friend. Just tell Jesus what you need. The only thing to remember, we have no authority to ask for anything except in Jesus' name. You always end your prayers saying, 'In the name of Jesus.' Okay?"

Suddenly, thinking about the sentencing coming up so soon and needing still another couple of minutes with someone with whom I could talk, I called, "Hey, Chaplain Firth?"

He returned. "Was there something else?"

"Yeah, well, one thing. I'm going up for sentencing Friday. I—would you—I mean, would you have time to say just one brief prayer for me? I mean, I know I deserve to have the book thrown at me, but—well, at least could you ask God to let me take it without breaking up?"

Chaplain Firth grinned and reached through the bars and patted me on the shoulder. "I'll be glad to pray for you, Don. I'm convinced you've truly repented for what you've done. I think Jesus will take that into consideration." He paused for a minute, then said, "If you really want to learn to use the language pleasing to God, read Psalms. David knew how to pray."

I went back to my bunk and picked up the Bible. I read most of the verses in Psalms, feeling a deep reverence raising me to a state of ecstasy, despite the grim ordeal to come.

With this boundless feeling, that night I embarked on a prayer marathon that lasted more or less till morning. I'd sleep a while, then awake and pray. Pray, then sleep. It was the strangest night in my life. I totally committed myself to Jesus and prayed with the most sincerity I'd ever felt. "Oh, Jesus," I said at one point, my voice trembling, "I'm just yours to use! Whatever you want for me, that is what I want."

Praying took me completely away from my surroundings. I felt as if I were drifting into space. "Lord," I said at another point, "Oh, Jesus, I *do* ask you for my freedom. I'll serve you in or out of jail but—oh, Jesus!—I *do* ask you for my freedom."

I'd pray in this way for a while, then feel I was asking too much and wonder whether to apologize to Christ for wanting more than I deserved. "Thy will, O Lord, be done. In Jesus' name. Amen," I finally said just before I dropped off to a sound sleep an hour or two before daylight.

When we marched down the street again towards the courthouse, I was hardly aware of the chains and the stares. I remembered Jesus walking through the village with the cross on His back and the crown of thorns on His head, and the jeers of the crowd. I wasn't so presumptuous as to compare myself with Jesus. I'd sinned. I'd been a creep for nearly half my life.

145

But I did feel if Jesus, who hadn't even sinned, could have endured this *unjust* punishment, then, in the similar circumstance, I could bear up under it.

In the courtroom, as people milled about and attorneys consulted with their clients, a tall guy came over to my group of prisoners. "Which one is Musgraves?" he asked.

I cleared my throat. "Here!"

"Yeah, well, I'm Clint Robens. I'm a court-appointed probation officer." He hesitated. He stared at me, his brow knitting. 'I've got to give a recommendation to the judge." Then he studied the paper he was holding in his hand. "Uh, your record doesn't look too good, Musgraves," he said looking up again. He paused some more, looking at the paper, then at my face. He licked his lips. "Musgraves," he finally said, slowly, "I don't know . . . your record is really something else again. But, you know, for some reason, I feel I should . . . Listen, Musgraves. . . ."

By now, I was practically dying. What was going on, anyway? Why was this guy so shaken up?

"If you got another chance," he finally said, "after you serve the remainder of your present six months' sentence, do you think you could go home to your family and live right?"

I had written Loris twice that week. I hadn't told her I had met the Lord, but I did hint I was different. "Something has happened to me inside," I'd said. "Loris, believe me—I think a miracle has occurred, and if you do take me back, we can make it."

The morning dragged on with case after case, the judge whipping out years, months, fines, and my case still not mentioned. I watched that judge bearing down on each guy as though he were a leftover from the French Revolution.

We had a couple of recesses, lunch. Finally, in mid-afternoon, my case came up. And it was over almost before it started. Robens, the probation officer, stood up with me in front of that hoary old judge with the tired grey eyes. "I recommend this man's sentence run concurrent with the one he's serving . . . that he be given additional probation but no additional time."

The judge nodded and handed a paper to the clerk.

Talk about miracles!

When I got back to the cell, I wrote another letter to Loris, still not telling about finding Jesus but exuding even more confidence in the changes that had taken place within me.

Buoyed up by the unexpected break in court, I was able to survive the weekend. I kept myself occupied reading the Bible. I couldn't get enough of the Bible. I started from Genesis and read through the Old Testament, then started again on the New.

Suddenly, it was Monday. And Sammy handed me a letter from Loris. I tore it open oblivious to staring eyes, and read it. The letter had been started the previous Wednesday, the same day that, unknown to Loris, I'd read John 3:3, knew what to call my experience, and quit smoking—and as I recalled now, her birthday:

Dear Don,

I've just finished reading your letter for the third time.

None of the things you've said in your letters, are, or sound, ridiculous. I know you have much time to think, but all of the thinking and determination you have now, while you're locked up, doesn't mean very much. It's what you do when they let you go that will tell the story.

You mentioned meeting me at the train station eight long years ago. I remember, too, how much I had missed you and how good it was to have your arms around me again. Yes, I loved you. And two years ago when I met you in Riverside after a long bus trip—you were unshaven, dirty and haggard. You'd just come off one of your high living drunks. I loved you then, too, so very much; and that night at the bar . . . I don't know what compelled me to go in there after you. I knew you wouldn't come home. Or maybe I should say, I knew you *couldn't* come home.

There was another night I'll never forget. The night I woke up to find you in our bedroom sneaking your clothes out. I wanted to scream and holler and beg you to stay but I didn't. I knew you *couldn't* stay and I knew why.

Sometimes I think I know you and understand you better than you do yourself. You couldn't come home to me and stay that night and many other nights because you felt unworthy of me and your children. You told me that night, "I'm a drunk and I can't live here any more," and so I let you go—and you were absolutely right, you are a drunk and you can't live with us any more.

147

Thursday 3/2/67

What makes you so sure you can pull yourself up out of it this time? What's so different about this time from all of the other times? It's not that I've lost all faith in you and I haven't given up on you completely, but I can never take another chance on you.

I don't hate you as much as you may think. My one big weakness is and always has been you, Don. I love you now and I always will. Isn't it a shame, though, that love isn't enough; anyway, it doesn't seem to be enough for us, does it?

I could go on loving you and waiting for you for the rest of my life, but if you don't succeed in changing yourself, what good will it do me to keep waiting for you? I don't intend to spend the rest of my life alone, Don.

I don't like living this way. It's very unnatural. It's not good for me and it's not good for the kids. I want and need a husband and they need a father. If you're not going to fulfill our needs, then I must find someone who will. I've made up my mind. I'm not going to raise these children by myself and I'm not going to spend the rest of my life working like this and miss out on being a mother to my children. They only see me a few hours a day. Tracy cries and screams and will hardly let me out of her sight for a minute for fear I'll leave her. I've missed all of Tracy's babyhood and most of Lynne's, and it's all your fault. I've never been ready to make a complete break from you, but I'm just about ready for it now.

Friday 3/3/67

I'm too tired to think. I need my sleep, will finish this tomorrow.

Saturday 3/4/67

Did you enjoy seeing Dick? He came by for a while this afternoon. What happened Friday in court? I called to find out what your sentence was for non-support. I was told you'd be out 7/1/67. Before, when I called about the bad check charge, I was told you had been given six months. That would mean you'd be out 6/1/67. Would you be kind enough to explain this to me, and will they make you serve the full sentence or will they let you go early?

I would so very much like to be able to say you could come home, but of course, I can't now, and I don't know whether I'll ever be able to. Even if you were to sober up, pay all of your debts and show you could assume some responsibilities . . . even if the miracle you spoke of should happen . . . how do either of us know it would last?

If the day ever comes when you're able to offer me all the things you've spoken of in your letter, if that day ever comes, I pray I'll be ready to make the right decision.

There are times when I want and need you, but if we are ever to share our lives together again, it will be only when I'm sure you are strong enough and can live the rest of your life in *my world*! Not your pretend world! If you still want to be "Mr. Big," and play "let's pretend," then go ahead. But if you do, you'll miss out on something you can never have again. You will never be able to have with someone else what you and I have had. No one else could ever love you the way I do, and nowhere else could you ever receive all of the many rewards which come from the children who love you.

I'll close now. I won't be writing to you again. It's better for me if I don't.

Let me know what they plan to do with you.

Loris

I was only momentarily shaken. Someone stood beside me, encouraging me. But, I certainly knew now what opposition Jesus and I would have to overcome in the next few months, yet I felt confident *we* would do it!

How strange—to be so confident after another letter that seemed to dash all my hopes, and negate that miracle in the courtroom!

But this was the way I was feeling lately. Bars, stone walls, and chains, obscenities, threats, the world's scorn, Loris' rejection—none of these things had the power to crush me. I was above it all.

I was above it, not in the sense of being self-righteous, but in having supreme faith in Jesus Christ, the Son of God, and His power over lives, His forgiveness of sin, His absolutely overwhelming love.

Another thing should have disturbed me mightily: I still hadn't been tried or sentenced for violation of Los Angeles County probation for the pre-Hawaiian heist; I could easily be ordered to serve out the remainder of that five-year term in San Quentin. Nor had I been tried for violation of the Dyer Act; nor for defrauding an innkeeper.

I attempted to forget this fact, but, every few days some cell mate in the jail would mention an escapade that called to mind one of my offenses.

During the next few weeks, I studied the Bible seriously, taking notes, writing questions. Each time the chaplain came, I would whammy him with a long list of questions. He finally got tired of answering them and gave me a book titled, *Halley's Handbook of the Bible.* This book answered most of my questions.

Many of my questions were of a historical nature, to help me place the events narrated in proper perspective.

There was one question, however, that neither the book nor Chaplain Firth could answer to my satisfaction. In Acts 2:1-4, I read, "When the day of Pentecost had come, they [the disciples] were all together in one place, and suddenly a sound came from heaven like the rush of a mighty wind, and filled all the house where they were sitting. And there appeared to them tongues as of fire, distributed and resting on each of them. And they were all filled with the Holy Spirit and began to speak in other tongues, as the Spirit gave them utterance."

The Scriptures continue describing this experience and mention other gifts of the Holy Spirit: healing, prophecy, visions, casting out demons, and supernatural defense against oppression and affliction.

To help other people by healing their minds and bodies and to be able to see more clearly into the future as to what God planned for mankind would be wonderful. It would be tremendous to be able fully to express one's feelings of love through tongues or, rather, to allow God to speak through my own mouth.

It would be great to be able to ask Jesus whether a particular plan was "right" with God. Dave Wilkerson evidently had had the gift of the Holy Spirit, I thought, because in his book he had a way of asking the Lord questions and receiving definite answers—of being able to pray for specific things and have those prayers answered and the deeds accomplished.

There is a progression to Christianity, I sensed. First, you come to know the Lord. You commit your life to Him. You learn to pray and have your prayers answered. I'd actually stumbled on this, in having my sentence reduced!

I felt I'd been lucky that first time in tapping this great reservoir of prayer power, but it seemed there was a definite formula, so to speak, whereby I could repeat the same kind of thing easily and with full confidence every time, if I just knew *how*.

The idea of supernatural *power* was implied in the verses pertaining to the Holy Spirit, a power you could use surely and tellingly *every time* if you could just get it.

I had gone up two steps of the ladder towards Jesus, having met Him, then committed my life to Him. I was groping for the next two or three steps.

The following Sunday, I attended the services as I'd been doing since I'd been born again and, when the services were over, I walked up to the altar, carrying my Bible, opened to Acts, and said, "Chaplain Firth. I'd like to ask you a question."

"Hey, Don," the Chaplain answered, "that's fine. What's your question?"

"Well, see here, where it says they were all filled with the Holy Ghost and they began to speak in tongues?"

"Yeah?"

"When is it going to happen to me?"

Chaplain Firth cleared his throat. "Well, Don, the way I've always interpreted that particular part of the Bible is those special powers were given to the apostles to help them get started. You must realize the Church was just beginning. There was a terrific amount of opposition, and God gave them these special gifts to enable them to survive long enough until they'd converted enough people to get going." He sighed. "I realize there is some controversy about these passages, but all I can say is what I personally feel."

I walked away disappointed. I still felt it would be marvelous to have that happen to me, to have the same power in me that was in Jesus when He was here in the flesh. I knew from my reading that Peter had been a perfect clod before he got filled with the Holy Spirit, a clod like me, bumbling along, sometimes reaching that pitch of reverent ecstasy where I could actually grasp the reins of that power briefly—through sheer happenstance.

But the power had transformed Peter. Why couldn't I have it, too? I had a hunger for the Holy Spirit every time I read the Book of Acts—a hunger that wouldn't quit.

151

Chapter 15

To make up for my disappointment and frustration, I began to testify in earnest to inmates, especially new ones. I could use my own voice, if not God's, to help other people and to share the great joy I did feel even when it fell short of the final, crowning grace.

Within another month, I had established quite a reputation in the Orange County Jail. Almost everybody knew something had happened to me. They knew when I prayed, things would happen.

One of the "miracles" I accomplished was helping Chaplain Firth fill the benches in the chapel. By now I had become acquainted with another guy in my cell block, Doug Blackwell, who also knew Jesus. Until I'd made myself conspicuous, he had kept his attitude to himself.

We were the only two who consistently went to Sunday services. We talked about this and decided we would pray, with the expectation the prayer would be fulfilled, asking that the benches be filled the following Sunday. In a corner of the cell block, we quietly began, praying by the blood of Jesus and by the power of the Spirit in His name.

That night, when everyone else was asleep, I repeated the prayer: "Jesus, Doug and I and Chaplain Firth want to do your work. We would ask you to fill that chapel this Sunday. We are without power except through you, Lord. The men here need you. We leave it in your hands, in Jesus' name. Amen."

Even though I had tried very hard really to believe our prayers would be answered, I was amazed Sunday when man after man crept nervously in and quietly sat down.

I could hardly wait until the next Sunday to see if it happened again. It did.

Meanwhile, people would come to me and get me to one side and stammer such words as, "Hey, Musgraves. I, er, uh, heard you're willing to pray for people." The guy'd laugh nervously and look around. "Well, anyway, I tried to believe in God a long time ago. Maybe there is such a thing, after all. If there is, I sure could use a favor right now."

I'd smile, "Sure, there's a God. He's right here in this cell, man. What do you want me to ask *Him*?"

And lots of times, these guys would come back after their day in court, or after they had talked to their wives during visiting hours, and would shake my hand and want to give me something—money, cigarettes, anything. "You did it!" they'd shout, this time making no secret of our arrangement.

I refused to accept any rewards. It wasn't I doing something: it was Jesus Christ.

By the approach of my fourth month, I had been responsible for at least four people actually coming right out and confessing Christ as their personal Saviour. I was so new at it myself, yet I'd been instrumental in *saving* four people from eternal damnation!

I was beginning to feel I could actually do something to make up for the rotten things I had done in my "other life." I was more and more eager to share Jesus.

Another evidence of power was the effect it had on the Number One Tough Guy in our cell block, Sammy. One time a prisoner came in and, within ten minutes of his initiation into our company, Sammy had knocked him to the floor, where he lay with his arms across his face, and Sammy ready to boot him one on the side of the head.

Without even thinking that no one, but no one, gets in Sammy's way—Sammy, the Satan-possessed with a killer's instinct—I jumped up from where I was sitting on the floor and wedged myself between the two of them. "That's enough," I said quietly.

Sammy stepped a pace back and stared at me as if he'd been hit by a thunderbolt. No one stopped Sammy. I stared right back at him. When he finally looked away momentarily, I, too, shifted my gaze. A dozen guys in that cell block were eyeballing me as though I were in a sideshow. I saw I was being measured for a coffin.

Sammy's fists were clenching and unclenching as he stared at me again, his eyes blinking, his mouth twitching. Then, suddenly, he just dropped his eyes, turned around, and strolled away.

The guy he'd beaten up was crying on the floor. He was bleeding and obviously badly hurt. Someone had already called the guards but, while waiting for them, I knelt and tried to make him comfortable and reassure him. I said, "You know, Jesus loves you. Just pray, and He'll take care of you. He changed my life while I was here."

"Yeah," he moaned. "Maybe Jesus changed your life, but that guy's going to take it for helping me. Just see. Tonight—or the next night. . . ."

"I'm not afraid, kid," I said. "I trust the Lord."

By now, the guards had opened the door. A guy examined him, then turned to the other. "Hospital case, Mac." He turned back to the injured man. "You better be more careful about slipping and falling like that. You could kill yourself."

"But I didn't—"

A chorus of "Shhhhhhhhhhs" went up around him, to remind him, YOU DON'T SQUEAL.

The incident put me in a new light. Up till now, only a few of the inmates actually believed my prayers for their cellmates had worked, that I had anything special—a hot line to Christ.

Now everyone regarded me with a certain deference. I was spared the crude jibes and practical jokes. I seemed to be set apart. Even the guards showed a new respect.

And even Sammy would look at me out of the corner of his eye. He knew there was something strange, forbidding about me, as far as he was concerned. He also knew I was no longer afraid of him. He even put me down on the list when he made up the handball teams for our weekly hour in the courtyard. He put me on his team. An unspoken relationship had sprung up between us.

My heart pounded with the hope that this meant someday, in some way, Sammy, the toughest guy in the cell and the one most possessed by Satan, would find the Lord.

Fired by the feeling of power and love, and satisfaction that I was having some effect on the lives of my cellmates, I searched the Scriptures to learn more about what was happening in this jail. I was lying on my bunk when John 15:16 hit me right between the eyes: "You did not choose me, but I chose you and appointed you that you should go and bear fruit and that your fruit should abide, so that whatever you ask the Father in my name, he may give it to you."

In Acts 1:8 Jesus had said, "You shall be my witnesses."

The two scriptures and others taken together seemed to indicate to me that by certain signs, Jesus would let us know who He has chosen to witness for Him. Well, the wonders that had occurred made it clear: He had chosen *me.*

"I have been chosen to minister for Christ," I announced to Chaplain Firth. I explained the basis for this conclusion.

He looked at me and sighed. "Don, I think you really have been called to witness. But to actually be ordained— a guy with your background—to stand in the pulpit and preach . . ." He spread his hands. "Don, I really can't see how you'd swing it." He smiled. "I know you're all excited about being born again, Don. But don't get your hopes up about getting into the ministry. You can be satisfied, can't you, to share the Lord at every opportunity? Don, there is a lot of schooling you would need, and most ordaining boards wouldn't look too favorably on your past."

I let his words sink in for several days. But I remained unconvinced. I felt such a strong calling to minister in a big way. I felt so much the power to change people, it was hard to believe I would not be able to do something about it when I got out of jail.

Sometimes, I wondered why Chaplain Firth's discouraging words didn't bother me. It was just as it had been with the chains, the bars, the concrete walls, the presence of violence and Satan as cellmate with me, and the knowledge that I hadn't heard from the authorities about the other three charges. Almost every week I'd sent notes to the "office" asking—and gotten no answers.

Then I finally heard about the violation of probation.

My Los Angeles Probation Officer came to the Orange County Jail to visit me and discuss the disposition of that case.

His attitude amazed me. During the time since I'd been given five years' probation, I'd been up and down and should have been in jail four or five times. Each time, the guy had given me a break. He sat, staring at me, and murmuring, "Musgraves, I don't know what's with you. I don't have any answers for you, but I wish I did. I suggest you go ahead and let me violate you. That is, I should go ahead and declare you have violated your probation. You might be lucky and draw only six months. That way, you wouldn't have to pay restitution."

"Wait a minute!" I said, incredulous. "Let me get this straight. Are you actually giving me a choice? I mean, you're leaving it up to me?"

He grinned. "I don't know why, Musgraves, but, yeah, that's it."

"Well, what *is* the other alternative?"

"The other alternative? I'll reinstate you. That means you'll be on all the probation you were on up to the time you got sentenced here, on this bum check rap—." He nodded thoughtfully. "But it means you're still liable for restitution. I just can't believe you'd make it, Musgraves. You'll be lucky if you get a job. And, if you go very long without making restitution payments, that's it! Back in jail. San Quentin."

"I'll get a job. Once I'm out of here, I'll make it."

He stared at me. "You sound pretty sure of yourself."

He cleared his throat. He probably thought I was stir crazy. "Well, anyway, so you'd like me to reinstate you? It'll be your last chance—"

"I won't need any more," I said. "And thank you."

"Yeah, well, okay. It's your neck, Musgraves. I'll have a letter sent to you officially stating this agreement—and a copy recorded in Los Angeles."

Another miracle.

It was a miracle in more ways than one—because it meant once I was released, I'd be on probation in two different counties . . . that right now, I was on probation in one county and serving time in another. It was just slightly unusual.

I continued to wonder about what action was going

156

to be taken on the remaining two counts and almost daily I expected a visit from FBI agents on the Dyer Act deal. But nothing happened.

All this time, I had been corresponding with Loris and the kids. I had answered Loris' letter which had cast grave doubts on my ability ever to lead a normal life by coming out strong with the fact I had actually met and accepted Jesus and had committed my life to Him. In subsequent letters, I gave her a day-by-day account of my spiritual experiences.

Her first letter in answer to this was still doubtful. She wrote,

March 9, 1967

Dear Don,

I feel the need to write you, but I don't quite know what to say. It's difficult to believe this religious experience such as you've described is happening to you—you, who as hard as you tried, could never make contact with God. I know you tried. Maybe you tried too hard. It was always so hard for you to accept something you couldn't understand, and Christ seemed to have no meaning or place in your life. Even after taking instruction in the church, I knew you hadn't really accepted it. I knew you wanted and needed it desperately, but it just didn't come.

And now this has happened to you . . . forgive me but I don't understand it. Please make me understand, Don, please make me understand.

Every time I read that letter it becomes clearer and more meaningful, but again I have to ask you, why do you think or how do you know you can keep this?

Temptation never ceases and you are so weak about certain things.

I must close now. Write soon.

Loris

I didn't let Loris' doubts worry me. I wrote an answer to her letter that very day.

I was overjoyed about a week later when Loris came through, at last, with an indication of restored faith and trust. It was another miracle, for sure!

March 13, 1967

Dear Don,

I just received your letter and finished reading it. It

moved me to tears. I love you so very much. It still astonishes me, the letters you write . . . the ease and freedom of thought that you put on paper. All of these things you convey to me, it helps so much. It's funny, the long period of time and distance which has separated us. It hasn't changed the way I feel about you. I love you now as much or even more than I ever did. I feel closer to you now than I ever thought possible.

When I used to pray for you so long and hard (before Lynne was born and when she was a baby), I never dreamed my prayers would be answered like this; but then when you do something, you really do it. I have to confess this bothers me a bit. The way you soar from one extreme to the other—from the depths of despair to exultation. You never seem to find a middle level. You're either way down or way up in the clouds.

I guess it's all right, just so long as you stay the way you are now, and keep growing in faith and understanding. I'm still not convinced it will last. God doesn't talk to me like He does to you. I guess that's because I don't talk to Him as much as I should. I usually fall asleep while I'm saying my prayers. I should make more of an effort to stay awake, even though He knows what's in my heart and what I want to say.

You know, I think it will be very difficult for me when you get out. We won't be able to get married again for a long, long, time. It was always hard for me before when I was around you. I don't know how to be friends with you, because I've always been your wife. Am I worrying about things I shouldn't?

I must close for now.

Love,
Loris

Three days after Independence Day, on July 7, I exploded in pure joy. With Jesus dwelling in my heart, I was overflowing with happiness. None of the usual delays in the processing routine could faze me. I waited patiently as papers were made out.

When the officer in charge was stapling papers together, I shot a glance at the rap sheet on his desk, the one recording my various charges and the disposition of my case. I was still bewildered by the complete lack of information on those two other counts.

Two bold red lines went down the middle of the sheet,

crossing out everything including the other counts. Red? Why red? Any color would have done as well. It made me think this was another physical manifestation: the blood of Jesus Christ had atoned for my sins. I was a free man at last. Free at last!

When I went into the last outer room leading to freedom, two uniformed men stepped my way. Their uniforms were slightly different from the police and guards I knew here, and on their badges were the initials LACS—Los Angeles County Sheriff. "Don Musgraves?" one asked.

He produced handcuffs. "You're under arrest. Violation of probation, Los Angeles County. Section. . . ."

As they put the bracelets on me, the other one said, "Will you accompany us to Los Angeles, please?"

I looked down at my manacled wrists. "Well, I'll be closer to the keys that way," I murmured.

A few months ago, such a turn of events would have floored me. I knew I had that letter confirming my probation had been reinstated. Still, I couldn't be sure at this moment whether some legal technicality had invalidated it. I should have been shaking like a leaf.

Instead, I walked straight and tall and confident between the two of them, down the steps toward the street. There was someone else squeezed in between me and Shorty. He was Officer Jesus Christ.

Chapter 16

"It's Daddy, it's Daddy!" one of the children screamed as I pushed open the gate to the apartment complex where Loris and the children now lived. Was this "little" Mike? He had changed and grown so much in a year and a half!

I hesitated for a minute, then held out my arms and swooped him up. "Hey, there, boy . . . Praise the Lord! *It is me!*" I hugged him tightly and he started to cry.

"Come on, now . . . let's have some smiles," I coaxed, trying to keep from breaking down myself. "Lynne and Tracy want a hug, too." I set Mike down and picked both girls up at the same time, surprised by their weight. Tracy began to scream.

"Don!" It was Loris, dressed in shorts (that showed off her tan) and one of those T-shirt tops.

Loris picked up Tracy and brought her back to me. We hugged each other, trying to get in a kiss with Tracy pushing on me and pulling on Loris.

"Oh, Tracy!" Loris cried. "Wait a minute, Don. She's too excited. I'll put her in her room."

"I'll come with you," I said, not wanting her out of my sight.

"I was just about to put her to bed, anyway . . . after I finished the dishes. I thought you'd be here earlier—in fact, I'd almost given up for the night."

"There was a mix-up and I had to go the L.A. you-know-what." I went on, "Because my probation officer forgot to leave word about the disposition of my case. They made some phone calls, so it all worked out!" I didn't want to say anymore in front of the kids. I recalled the panic I'd felt until I remembered Jesus was walking with me now . . . I wasn't alone anymore. He had meant for me to take that detour, just as a last reminder.

It took us all about an hour before we could get used to each other. The joy in the room as we all sat together, a family again for the first time in eighteen months, was just what I had pictured while in jail, especially precious because now Jesus was head of this family. I was a lucky man. God had given me one more chance to see what I had almost thrown away. As the kids chattered, I murmured, "Thank you, Jesus."

"I hope my letters weren't too discouraging, Don." Loris hesitated. She took a deep breath. "I had to let you know I was at the end of my rope. We couldn't go on anymore unless you really changed." She looked hard at me. "You have changed, haven't you?"

"Believe it, honey. Jesus entered my heart. He won't let me down."

"It really broke me up to have to write like that but I was really hurting . . ." Her voice broke. "The Lord had put a deep faith in me that things would work out eventually. I didn't want anyone else for a husband. I was just waiting for God to do something."

"Look, honey, you don't have to explain. I know what a heel I've been. But I've got Jesus now."

"Yes, I know," Loris agreed. She looked at me as though really seeing me for the first time. "You are different!"

We talked on and on. Each time one of us mentioned a problem, the other would come up with an answer or tentative solution. I felt as though Jesus were sitting right there with us, telling me what to say, helping me win back the one true love I'd ever had.

It was really rough parting. But Loris had divorced me—legally, we were no longer man and wife—and Loris' parents were still opposed to me. My mother had invited me to live at her house until I got on my feet and Loris and I were remarried. I thought it would be wiser if we kept it this way until I had worked for a while, paid off some back bills and started to save money. Loris would continue working, too, until the situation looked better. Everyone would have time to accept our reconciliation.

We kissed good night and Loris clung, not wanting me to go anymore than I wanted to leave.

Freedom! It was a blessing. It also had its comical moments. Even after such a relatively short time of being locked up, I had almost forgotten how to get along in the world. At intersections, I had to re-think the procedure for crossing the street: look for the green light, look to the left, then right, then start crossing.

It was the same way with driving. After all the cross-country driving I'd done, I still had to get used to the *timing* again, and estimating distances in relation to slowing down and stopping.

I stopped by almost every evening to have dinner with Loris and the kids. We went to church and Sunday school together, and Wednesday evening prayer meeting. We attended Loris' church.

Meanwhile, I was having trouble finding employment. No longer inclined to falsify application forms or lie to personnel managers, I felt the full force of the prejudice on the part of employers against hiring ex-convicts.

While still in jail, I'd gotten the impression God had nixed restaurant work because so much of my sinful past was tied up with it. Whatever I'd do, I would have to start from scratch.

But my new ability to be humble and go God's way helped. That, and prayer. I finally wangled a job driving a laundry truck, picking up people's dirty clothes. It paid me just enough to get by on.

What was so amazing was all these problems seemed so trivial! The most agonizing thing about those months was seeing Loris only for those brief moments we could be together, and having to leave her just when I wanted to grab her in my arms.

I don't think I could have taken it if the love of Jesus hadn't lifted my heart. I lost myself in prayer—though sometimes tears would overflow while I prayed. "Thy will be done," I said—"but I sure hope your will is for this, too, to pass quickly."

Because of this overflowing love for Jesus Christ, my

overwhelming gratitude for what Christ had done for me, and the Bible's exhortation to witness, I didn't know how to contain myself. I was so fired up about Jesus and so full of love, I lost all reason when it came to dealing with other people.

What do you say to a crusading laundry man as he hands you your laundry, and starts spouting about Jesus Christ and His ability to make you pure again? "You have to be washed in the blood of the Lamb" was one of my pet opening wedges.

But one of my customers got the last laugh on me. Every Monday morning, I had to stop by the Anaheim Christian Center (now Melodyland Christian Center). The thing which puzzled me about this customer was that the laundry always consisted almost entirely of *wet robes*— about fifty of them, every Monday morning, rain or shine.

Finally, after several weeks I got up enough nerve to ask, "What gives with these wet robes, anyway?"

"We baptize Christians," Associate Pastor Glen Anderson answered, looking at me as though I should have known.

"Oh." That was all I could say. What church could baptize fifty people a week these days? Maybe fifty in a *year* would be more like it.

Most customers accepted my wild witnessing with good humor. It was a different matter at the Lutheran church in Orange where Loris, the kids, and I went every Sunday.

Bless their hearts, they were friendly and they accepted my return. But when I cornered any of their members and started telling them how much Jesus had done for me, one by one they would back off.

One Sunday, Loris and I were listening to the opening prayer when I noticed the smell of alcohol wafting from a man behind us. When I got a chance to, while the pastor was saying something about the urban crisis, I looked over my shoulder and smiled. I wanted to say right then and there, "Jesus love you." But I controlled myself until we were leaving.

As he started down the steps, I grabbed his arm. "Man, do you know what God has done for me?" I asked.

He moved away but I hurried after him.

163

"Wait!" I hollered. "I've got to tell you—the Lord wants me to tell you He can deliver you from your alcohol problem!"

"Don," Loris put her hand on my arm and whispered. "People are staring. Come on."

The only discomfort Loris and I felt in each other's company was this difference in the way we felt about expressing our Christianity. Since Loris had always gone to this church and knew everyone, it was agony for us both. I'd have to retrain myself from saying out loud, "Praise the Lord," or "Hallelujah."

I couldn't see the humor in all this at the time. I kept asking Jesus, "What am I doing wrong? Why do I turn everyone off when I try to bring them your message?" I prayed for help.

Another thing weighing heavily on me was my failure to find anyone who could explain why the baptism of the Holy Spirit was a thing of the past.

I must have read Acts, chapter 2, a hundred times and still could not believe it didn't apply to the present. All these people ribbing or snubbing me ... everyone blind to Jesus' supernatural gifts. Was I off base?

After a few months, I quit the laundry job. I was too preoccupied to build up the route. I went to a print shop in Anaheim. That was one thing I could do, although I knew it would be boring. It was close to where Loris lived and the pay was better.

In my quest for knowledge, I joined the Anaheim chapter of the Christian Businessmen's Committee, and I began to pester them with all of my questions.

I had been reading more about the Holy Spirit, but I still hadn't met anyone who could tell me enough about it. One morning at the meeting, I brought up the subject again. "Is this something that just the Christians of the 'olden days' received?" I looked around at the different faces, but all I drew was blank stares. "You men are all deep, faithful Christians. I know, because I can feel the Lord is here, with us, right in this room. But, why don't any of you know about the gift of God's Holy Spirit?"

Jack Gutman was motioning for me to sit down. Saturday morning he called me on the phone.

"Yeah, look Jack," I said, "I'm sorry if I disturb people, but I'm serious about wanting to learn about the baptism. I thought it would be the perfect place to find out, after all . . ." I sensed he knew more than he was saying. "Say, do you know anything about it?"

"Yes, Don. That's why I called," he answered. "Look, are you busy right now?"

"Not too busy to talk with you."

"Why don't you come on over to my house and we'll discuss it further?"

Jack was waiting for me on his front porch.

"Don, I received the baptism of the Holy Spirit two weeks ago."

"You, *what*?"

"I've had to hide it because I decided to stay in my own church. I'm a Baptist. But whenever those gifts appear, I know He is there, right with them."

"You mean, you knew what I was looking for all this time, but you didn't say anything?" I exploded.

"Calm down, now." He laughed. "God had a function for you. He has one for me. But you have to let Him tell you when He thinks you are ready for it. He will let you know, if you pay attention."

"But, I've always prayed . . . the Lord knows I want it," I stammered.

"I know that too, Don," he went on. "But it's not just something we can reach out our hands for and receive. You have to seek these gifts through prayer, and through increasing obedience to the teaching of the Spirit." He paused a minute to make sure I was taking all of this in. "Do you know how love is defined in the New Testament?"

"Well, I think so." I answered. "It's an emotion, a feeling, and a state of mind."

"You're partly right. It's all of those things, but for a Christian, it's a course of action!" Jack got up and paced the floor, then kind of shook his head as he walked back and forth. "God loved the world which He had created. When He saw that His creatures had gone astray, He acted. He sent His Son to manifest His love and to win the creatures back to harmony with the Creator. The Son, Jesus Christ, forgave sins, healed the sick, cast out demons, and proclaimed God's kingdom. By these acts of love He restored for those who will accept His love the lost harmony within man, between man and man, nation and nation, and between man and God."

"Love, you're talking about real LOVE, aren't you?" I asked. "When you think about it in those terms, it's overwhelming, isn't it? Not too many of us would even offer to die in place of a loved one."

"That's the kind of love we're talking about here, Don." This was the first time I had ever seen Jack so animated. "After we've done all these things against Him, He asks us to accept His love. It's twofold. First, we're supposed to accept these manifestations of His love—forgiveness for our sins, healing for our bodies, minds, and spirits, and deliverance from all forces of evil. Then we're supposed to act as His agents in bringing these manifestations of His love to others."

I nodded. I was thinking about God's love. I wasn't sure I deserved that much love. On our knees, Jack put his hands on me and started praying. He prayed in tongues, then he interpreted what he had said. Then we both prayed together.

We stayed on our knees for at least a half hour. Nothing happened. I thanked Jack and left, knowing he was as disappointed as I.

I was so brokenhearted, I started weeping. I couldn't stop. "Is there something still wrong with me, God?" I asked, on the way home. Why are you withholding this gift that is supposed to be ours, free?"

Chapter 17

Loris had worried and prayed about me while I was at Jack's. After struggling through dinner, hardly able to eat anything, I said, "Honey, I'm really sorry, but this thing bugs me like crazy. I know I'm close to receiving the baptism in the Holy Spirit, but it just won't come!"

"I know. It's all right." She smiled. "Go home and rest. We'll go to church together tomorrow. I'm sure it will happen to you soon."

Loris had always been a devout church-goer, and *her* identity with the Lord dated back to childhood, and was strongest during communion service. "At communion," she admitted, "I could feel God's presence so strongly I could hardly get up to go up front to take communion."

As I drove home that night, I kept thinking about Loris' experiences and about what Jack had said.

Alone in Mom's house—she'd gone to visit my brother Jim—and in a meditative mood, I sat on my bed to read some scriptures before calling it a night.

Just after ten o'clock, I knelt on the floor to pray. Mingling with my thoughts as I tried to formulate words of praise were all the things I had been reading and studying and thinking about the past few days. Especially the rapt expression on Jack Gutman's face when he'd laid his hands on me and prayed for me to receive the baptism in the Holy Spirit.

I had really challenged him. I started over again with my prayer, saying, "Dear Father...." Then what came bursting forth was a language I had never spoken or heard before. It was strange—but beautiful!

167

I knew at once this was what I had been seeking. It was possible, then, to receive it! God had merely been waiting for the right time to bestow his gifts. While still kneeling, I had a vision.

I was in the Holy Land. I was walking down a road. I looked up at a building and suddenly knew in the second story was the upper room! I went in. A shaft of light came through a window and I was standing in the middle of it, transformed. I raised my arms.

Every fiber of my body was super-generated! Power surged through me. Now . . . *now*! . . . *I* had the power Jesus wanted me to have.

"Oh, praise God!" I kept saying over and over and over, still talking in tongues. The flow of sonorous speech rolled off my tongue and enveloped me in a musical echoing full of glory and meaning.

I lost track of my surroundings. The living room was still the upper room and the light was no longer a beam coming at me from the outside, but a beacon inside me, golden and uplifting.

I got into bed but I didn't sleep. Every thought I had was clear and concise, as if I had thought it for the first time. I kept praying and praising God. By the time I got up the next morning, I felt a new freedom and power I'd never known.

Looking in the mirror as I shaved, I saw Don Musgraves, all right. But it wasn't the Don Musgraves of yesterday. *He* no longer lived here! I positively glowed with a visible light. I couldn't wait to pick up Loris and the children for church.

"Something's happened," Loris proclaimed when she opened the door.

I hugged her. "I received it! I got the baptism in the Holy Spirit last night."

"Oh, Don . . ."

"It was everything I thought it would be. And more. But . . ." I looked at her wonderingly. "How did you know something was different?"

"Your eyes . . . your face . . . I don't know, but—oh, Don, it's so wonderful. I'm so happy for you."

That morning in the Lutheran church was one of the most difficult times Loris and I had ever faced together.

We were sitting in the fourth row from the front, and every time the minister said something, I wanted to explode in joyous answer. Every time he bowed his head to pray, Loris would poke me to remind me to pray in silence.

The service seemed extra long. I was ready to erupt by the time we walked out. I was sure that everyone in that church could detect a difference in me. Coming down the steps I spotted Mr. Jenkins, who had once been a treasurer of the city of Orange. He was standing just a few feet away, looking for someone.

"Mr. Jenkins, did you hear about what happened to me last night?" I asked as I pulled Loris over closer.

"No, what?" he asked wearily.

"I received the baptism in the Holy Spirit, and now my whole life is changed."

He turned away again, peering up the street, then looked back at me. "That's really great, Don," he said unenthusiastically.

"Look," I said moving even closer to him. "I'll bet you don't even know what that means." I looked around at people who had gathered behind us. "I haven't heard of one person in this church who *has* received the baptism in the Holy Spirit." This brought a gasp from some of the women behind Loris.

"I don't see how you people can come to this church Sunday after Sunday and still not know the meaning of the baptism or really talking with the Lord. I guess Loris and I will just have to find a place where they do understand this."

Loris broke away and headed down the steps. This brought me to my senses, and I looked around at the people staring. No one said a word. I hurried after Loris.

"Oh, Don!" she cried, "I was afraid you were going to do that, even in the service."

During the next few weeks I made a concerted effort to restrain myself in public. In the meantime, Loris was becoming accustomed to my verbal way of showing my love for Christ. I suggested we visit other churches and she agreed.

One Sunday we visited a church in Garden Grove. The service started out like any other except the congregation took a larger part in responding to the minister. *Amen, hallelujah*, and *praise the Lord* boomed all around us and Loris began to get uneasy.

I felt right at home, however, and began to join in. Loris became more and more agitated, and I finally woke up to the fact, but we couldn't leave. A deep feeling was here, a presence. God was in that church.

Loris didn't say much on the way home. "Look, baby," I said after several minutes of silence, "I know that church was very different from the one we've been worshipping in. But I felt freer there. I wish I could explain."

"Oh, Don!" Loris almost cried. "I wish I could let loose like that, like you do, but I just wasn't brought up that way."

When we got back to the apartment, I tried to talk to her about leaving the Lutheran church and going somewhere else to worship. She was dead set against it, but she didn't want to upset me, either, so it was a bad situation. "Why can't I see the Lord the way you do? I don't have that joyful feeling all the time. Help me, Don. I want to be the way you are."

But we agreed to drop the issue.

The important thing was we had each other. She put her arms around me, loving me, leaning on me. *She* was *leaning* on me now! "When you come in at night," she said, "tired from working at that boring job of yours, the light comes right in with you. The whole room lights up with your presence! The children have noticed it, too. Why, look how Tracy runs to you now."

I laughed. It was marvelous to hear. Now that I had the baptism in the Holy Spirit, I thought anything and everything was possible. "Which brings up another question," I murmured. "Why don't we set the wedding date? This business of your being here and my being umpteen blocks away isn't good for you or the kids or me." I took her hand. "With the power of the Holy Spirit with us now, we are going to be a real team."

On January 26, 1968, Loris and I met at the Lutheran church. It was the same church at which we'd been married in 1957, eleven years before, when the sanctuary had been crowded with relatives and well-wishers.

On this occasion, there was only my brother Jim and

his wife and the minister—a different minister from the one who had married us before.

Oh . . . there *was* one other wedding guest: Jesus Christ. He made all the difference. This time we were united in Christ.

We went home and had a party with our three children and a few relatives. Loris and I knew we still had many problems to face, but now we could face them together as man and wife, and Jesus Christ was going to be our guide.

Soon after I moved into the small apartment in Orange, we began to pray to find a house. When we wanted to ask someone in to hear about the Lord or attend a prayer meeting, the tiny apartment was impossible.

After all, I thought, tongue in my cheek, didn't Jesus say He was preparing a place for us? I was thinking of John 14:2: "In my Father's house are many mansions, if it were not so, would I have told you that I go to prepare a place for you?"

We prayed every night for a solid month that God would give us a sign that we *could* buy a house. After thirty days, we felt He'd affirmed it and we could start looking. He would show us which one it was and we would be able to buy it.

"You're crazy!" some of our friends said. "You don't have any credit. If they investigate and find you have a record—"

"Yeah. I know," I cut them off. "But God wants us to have a house, and the kids deserve more room to play in."

We contacted a realtor in Garden Grove who had run some rather interesting ads about vacated houses which could be bought for a fair price. His office was just a little hole in the wall with pictures of houses plastered all over the front window. The minute I saw the guy, I knew he was a crook. It took a crook to know a crook. I felt comfortable with him—maybe because I knew what he was like.

The first house he showed us was a wreck. We shook our heads. "Surely, you have something more?"

He drove us all over the area, pointing out possibilities. We started in some pretty crummy neighborhoods;

now we were working up to some nicer ones. "How much is that one?" I asked, pointing to one which looked about our size.

He checked his book. "Around $18,000; want to look at it?" Before we could answer, he had pulled over. "It's got three bedrooms, and the yard is in pretty good shape."

By now Loris and I were able to size up a house pretty fast. It looked like the right one. Next to our apartment it was spacious. All the rooms were big.

At his office while he pulled out some papers, I bowed my head. "Lord," I whispered, "is this the house?" I got such a strong leading from that prayer, I felt it was right to go ahead. "Go ahead and start the processing for the house. The Lord has just said okay. But first, there are a few things I should tell you."

He looked up. "Yeah?"

For the next forty-five minutes I bent his ear, giving him my testimony. He sat back in his chair, amazed. When I was finished he shook his head.

"Frankly, Mr. Musgraves, after I put all that rubbish down on paper, I can't think of a loan company that would pick it up." He leaned back and lit a big cigar. "Do you really think your references will help that much?"

A week went by and we didn't hear from him. We prayed harder now, feeling this was the right house.

Ten days later he called. "They've had to raise the points, but if you still want it, I think I can get it for you." As if in fine print, he added, "It'll cost $150 more."

I didn't let him get away with that. "Look," I said. "God and I have a contract, too. That one we made out in your office more than a week ago, remember? We can't change it."

"God? We?" He was baffled.

"We—God and I—can't change it. That's that."

He hung up muttering.

"Well," Loris sighed. "You did it again."

"Yep. We'll never see him again," I agreed.

But we did. The following week he turned up waving

172

a paper in our face. "Well, for some reason, you can go ahead with the deal after all." Slumped on our sofa, he looked from Loris to me as if we were a couple of nuts. "I don't understand what's happening here."

Later, he telephoned. "We're running into some difficulties," he said. "Nine loan companies have turned you down. I guess we'd just better forget it."

"Forget it? After all this? Listen, God is determined we have that house. You'll just have to try a few more. We've been praying about it and there's no doubt. There is a way. God says so."

"After nine lenders have turned thumbs down? You've got to be—Ahhh, never mind. We'll go back through the phone directory."

This time it was a month before we were called on by Mr. Swain again. He brought another man with him, both looking in a mild state of shock. "It's incredible, but, well, Home Loan picked up your loan."

He hesitated. His companion, looking uneasy, coughed, then said, "Mr. Swain and I have something to tell you. There's a catch. The points are up, and we've got to have another $150 before we can swing the deal."

"Look," I sputtered, "I already went through that. God and I made a contract and we aren't changing."

They looked at each other, then Mr. Swain said, "We're only $150 away from a deal that seemed impossible from the word go."

His companion said, "I'll tell you what we'll do. We won't have to change the contract. Does your God object to someone who needs $150? The man and wife who own that house need it badly. She's *sick*."

"In that case, Loris and I will pray about it." I stood up. "We'll be back in a few minutes." Loris followed me into the bedroom. We bowed our heads and sought God's will. I don't know how long we were in the bedroom but when we came back out, the gentlemen had filled up a saucer with cigarette butts. "God says *go*," I said.

When Mr. Swain returned to finalize the deal, he shook my hand. "Mr. Musgraves, you mentioned this Christian

Businessmen's group. Uh, when they meet again, could I come with you? I want to see if there are any more like you."

At the next Friday morning meeting I introduced Mr. Swain. I don't think there has been anyone since who received a more direct witness right on the spot and anyone so willing to receive the Lord. God had put Loris and me into a house. It had taken five months—one of the longest escrow's on record—but we had made it. Five months isn't long for an impossibility.

After we moved in, I went on working and witnessing at the printers. One by one, I'd talk with the other employees about Jesus. One by one, I alienated them. I shared Christ with them, but they wouldn't have anything to do with Him. Or me. Finally, I found myself "brown bagging" it at lunch time alone. I used rap time to read the Bible.

One Monday morning, the customer who brought in brokerage business each week brought in his order—and his odor. He was wearing his usual bloodshot eyes. "Man, that was really a swinging party we had in the mountains this weekend," he said.

"I used to have those kind of parties, too," I mused. "And I used to smell like you do."

He didn't know me very well and I'd caught him off guard. His face got even redder.

"I used to be sick and hung over like you," I continued blithely, "and, one day, in the Orange County Jail, I met Jesus."

He exploded like a radiator pulling a trailer up a mountain in mid-summer. In a few short, impolite words, he told me to shut my mouth.

I went back to the multilith wondering why he'd taken it so hard—but also knowing I'd put a hook into him.

I was right. One day, after several weeks, he came into the room and we started talking about his problems.

I took him to the next Christian Businessmen's Committee meeting. He felt the experience so deeply he was saved right then and there and, afterwards, became a real leader in the CBMC, eventually going on to become the president of one of the new Orange County groups.

I finally quit the printers. Through CBMC I had met Cecil Conners who asked me if I'd be interested in taking over the field work for him, calling on new accounts and keeping up old ones in his salt business.

Loris and I were attending classes at the Christian Center Church Thursday nights. Christian Center was interdenominational in its ministry to the community. Pastor Ralph Wilkerson (no relation to Dave Wilkerson) was a young man with enthusiasm for the Lord. He was a sharp administrator as well. He picked people to work who were well qualified, who could bring results—for the Lord.

God kept speaking to me. Every day I was getting the feeling through prayer that I had an urgent calling to work for Him in a particular way. Along with this, I was really grabbed by the way the Christian Center was harvesting souls.

Fired up about it, I got nervous, fidgety. "I've got to be part of that program, Loris!" I shouted one day. "Praise God, those people are really with it!"

"They've got some top people there, haven't they, Don?" Loris replied. "I mean, maybe some day, after you have really proved yourself . . . "

I almost cried. Here was my own wife miserably failing to grasp what I was thinking. "Doesn't all the suffering I've had count for anything?" I cried. "I've got a lot those people don't have—actual experience of the kind of person they are trying to reach." I looked at Loris, trying to calm down and control my feelings. "Loris, don't I have enough fire? I mean, do you think I'm *still* holding back on God?"

Loris threw her arms around me. "Oh, Don, you *know* I don't mean that. It's not that at all. Why, you're so filled with the Holy Spirit that you—you *float!*"

"Well, then," I said, finally, pushing back and looking down at her with a smile. "That's all that matters. If *you* recognize it, surely Wilkerson will."

After Church Bible Class one evening, I knocked boldly on Pastor Wilkerson's office door.

"Come in," his voice called out absentmindedly.

"I'm—"

"Yes, yes?"

"Well, I just thought I'd stop by and tell you—"

"Tell me what?"

"Well, I'd like to work for you. I'd like to be on the staff—"

"To do what?"

I gulped, then shrugged. "Well, ah . . . I don't know."

Wilkerson studied me for a brief instant, then said, "Well, you'd better pray about *that* real seriously." He leaned back in his chair, looking right through me. Finally, he said, "Do you realize, I talk to a dozen people a week who say the same thing?"

I left the building as quickly as possible. I didn't want to talk to anyone. I was crushed. I'd gone into Wilkerson's office with all the confidence in the world that he would jump up from his chair, grab my hand and welcome me into the fold.

I cried as I got into my car. "Oh, Jesus, Lord! What *is* it you want me to do?"

I hadn't even stated my case in that office, stopped short by something in Pastor Wilkerson's eyes. Did he have the knack of seeing right through people, like God?

Was it because of my background that he'd been so curt? Being an ex-con had already held me back from many jobs. Was it going to go against me, instead of for me, in working for the Lord?

Meanwhile, I *was* involved in a "miniature ministry" at the Orange County Jail. Ever since my release, I'd been going every Sunday afternoon as kind of an unofficial "assistant" chaplain, bringing Jesus and a touch of companionship to inmates.

But I was severely limited in what I could do, and my energies were not concentrated to the point where I felt I was doing much good.

My heart wasn't in the salt business, either.

After several weeks, I went into Pastor Wilkerson's office again to plead for a place in his organization, for something to do to make me feel as though I were moving forward in Jesus. "To do what?" He asked again, adding, "The only possible chance you'd have would be to get some real solid Bible training. That takes time and money." He shook his head sadly.

I was really discouraged this time. "Lord," I prayed, "how in the world can a guy like me go back to college—to Bible college?" I wasn't earning enough at the salt company to do more than support my family on a subsistence basis and pay back those I'd wronged.

I made up a list of thirty reasons why I couldn't enroll in Bible school. My friends, Loris, and I prayed the Lord would consider this list of negatives and give us *His* will. And, miraculously, one-by-one, the things on that list began to disappear as solutions were offered.

Time was running out to make a decision about enrolling. In the prayer room at Melodyland Christian Center the last Sunday before this deadline, I talked with Sunday School Pastor Al Porterfield and we prayed together.

Then, early that week, I went ahead and enrolled for three classes at the Southern California College, in Costa Mesa.

I quit the salt company. Cecil suggested I try to get a job at a machine shop nearby.

"It's basically a sawing operation, cutting and filing steel, that sort of thing," owner George Donehowers explained. "The salary isn't tremendous, but you can work your hours in to suit your classes."

I asked for time to think about it. In the back of my mind, I had the feeling I should be making a lot more money—about $10,000 a year. As I procrastinated and lined up some appointments for job interviews, I had one pleasant experience. Loris had been moved by the Lord to agree to transfer our membership from the Lutheran church to Melodyland Christian Center.

I spent the next month driving all over Southern California chasing down job tips. Finally, an offer came through from Prudential Insurance with a salary of $10,000 a year. I had an interview with the supervisor in Los Angeles, during which he outlined the program.

It sounded real great. The only drawback was I would have to attend a lengthy training program back *East*.

That was a real curve! I put him off on a decision but did use some of the time to witness to him. "It sounds as though you have some deciding to do, Mr. Musgraves," he said. "Can we have your answer within the week?"

"I'll be praying about it, sir," I answered.

I felt so strongly I should continue with my Bible college studies in Costa Mesa and prepare myself for a ministry that the prospect of traveling back East for a lengthy training program turned me off completely. I told the personnel manager I had to decline his offer.

He breathed hard into the telephone. "Musgraves," he said, "you must be nuts."

After I hung up, I cried. Until that moment, that instant of finality, it hadn't dawned on me the awesome thing I had done.

I had turned down the job with the saw company. And I'd topped that by turning down a dignified executive-type position offering nearly $1,000 a month.

We had house payments to make, food and gas to buy, restitution payments—and only Loris' pay check coming in.

I'd really stuck my neck out.

I was trembling—tears streaming down my face. "Lord," I prayed, "I hope I've made the right decision. I've just turned down $10,000 a year to do your work."

Chapter 18

The bars from the window cast shadows slantwise across the men on the eight bunks. The door clanked open, another blue-denimed man stumbled in, the door clanked shut.

"Well, all I can say is, they didn't waste any time filling empty bunks." The fat-faced guy with the pig eyes laughed sardonically, "How long was that bunk empty, Charlie?" Charlie didn't answer. He turned to the newcomer, who seemed to know his way around a jail cell. "Back so soon?"

"Was we introduced?" the newcomer said, claiming his bunk and lying down with his hands under his head.

"I seen you in the handball court when I was here last year. We must've been out the same time. My name's Slim."

"Then, you put on some weight since," another prisoner commented. He was silent for a minute, then said, "I guess you could call me Ray. I don't remember seeing you here before and we won't have long to get acquainted. I expect a big book this time. A ticket to Q. Yeah, yeah, I know what you're going to ask. 'What you in for?' Well, I tried to go straight, but you got to eat and no ex-con's wanted in the classifieds. So I figures I might as well eat *big* and do it any way I could."

"You ain't in for nothing like drunk in auto, then, I take it," Slim commented.

"Maybe like carrying a torch for a safe?" one of the other of the assemblage of ten suggested.

"Your twenty questions is up," Ray said. "I played

enough guessing games with the cops. No, I just breezed into a liquor store to grab a fifth of something sweet. I saw I was alone with the clerk and decided to go for broke."

"Only, you weren't alone." The quiet guy on the top bunk at the end had put down the book he was reading.

"Jesus Christ wasn't in that liquor store with me, that's for sure," Ray replied. He yawned. "No. I thought I could get to the register by mugging the jerk. But he knew some karate. Just enough."

"Speaking of Jesus Christ . . ." I picked up the book Charlie had been reading. "It says in here, 'Even though I walk through the valley of the shadow of death, I will fear no evil; for thou art with me.'"

Charlie nodded. "Only that was in the Old Testament."

"Nevertheless," I said, "Jesus loves you. And He's with you all the time. You don't have to go looking for Him. He's right here in this cell with you."

Ray angled his head up to where I was standing and peered through the bars at me. "Hey, man, are you some kind of—?"

"Knock it off." Slim's voice was harsh.

"Yeah. This guy really has it," replied a cellmate nicknamed Third Man. "I don't know how he does it, but he fixes things."

"He's got a hot line to Somebody up there," another said. "I seen him operate. He comes around when a guy needs him. Charlie, here—." He gestured. "Wanted to crash for good even if he has to spend a little time before he has a chance to prove it. So, he sent for Musgraves."

"You mean, you're just visiting?" Ray looked baffled. "I wondered why you weren't in uniform." He thought a minute. "Just like that? You come and go when you want to?"

Third Man cleared his throat noisily. "Sometimes it almost seems like he comes right through the walls without even knocking."

I laughed. "You're my next target, Third. It *seems* like that because I feel so free. Jesus is with me and, well, it just makes me kind of float."

"Don't knock it, either. He sure helped me," Charlie

180

said. "You hear all this stuff about how, like, impossible it is to get off H? He got me off it in half a day."

Charlie had used the one phone call they'd allowed him to phone the church. He'd heard about us from some addict who was considering giving us a jingle. Charlie knew he was in for a bad withdrawal and, anyway, had been wanting to get off heroin for months. On the slight chance we could help, he called us.

The "we" was the Melodyland Christian Center. I'd finally made it! I was in the Intern Program, answering phones and running all over the place—to schools, jails, hospitals, homes, wherever someone was in trouble and wanted help.

It wasn't the first time I'd gone back to the Orange County Jail, either. Only a couple of months after my own release in 1967, I'd gone with Chaplain Jim Firth on his twice weekly visits to the jail.

At first I wondered whether I wouldn't feel uncomfortable going back to that dungeon. But, no: Jesus went with me and we had a ball.

In those cells crowded with eight bunks, there were ten of us when I went a'ministering: eight inmates, Don Musgraves, and Jesus Christ.

Even though most of the prisoners couldn't go the whole route with Jesus, they seemed to recognize I had special leverage with *Someone*, and they treated me with awed respect. And, I did help dozens of inmates relate to Jesus Christ.

I went the rounds on Sunday afternoons and Thursday evenings as an assistant to the chaplain.

One fellow, Jim Archer, came up to me one evening and told me he was there for manslaughter, for beating a man to death who had been having sexual relations with his wife. Jim expected to go to San Quentin for five years to life.

"Jesus can intervene for you," I assured him.

The man actually cried. We prayed together and Jim asked the Lord into his life. After that, there was a real change in him. He ended up getting sentenced to three years at Atascadero for psychological treatment. I kept tabs on him through correspondence. He became a leading figure in a Christian group at the institution.

Another experience had a direct influence on my first real ministry. I walked into the jail one Thursday night, said "hello" to the guard at the front gate, walked through two double steel doors, and when the second door clanged shut, heard a blood-curdling scream.

The hair on my neck stood up. "What is happening here?"

"We just booked a couple of teenagers for possession." He sighed and shook his head. "One of them decided to swallow the evidence. It was in a plastic bag."

"What's in it?"

He shrugged. "We don't know. He can't talk and his buddy's too spaced out to make sense. We're taking the sick one to the hospital right now."

I couldn't do a good job of counselling that night. Those screams kept ringing in my ear.

It haunted me the next few days. When I went to the jail the next time, I asked what had happened. "We were too late," the guard sighed tiredly. "He died."

God seemed to have led me to this experience. For many months afterwards, I'd feel the urge to get into a drug-prevention ministry. But the Lord was leading me along a path the destination of which was then unclear.

My successes inspired me to want to help inmates. I could identify with them, especially with their discouragement about getting jobs when released. I was having the same problem, trying to find a job with adequate pay.

And yet, before I made it at the Christian Center, I was having a *bunch* of problems and seemed to be making all the wrong decisions. I'd just started at the expensive Bible college, but I had the audacity to turn down two jobs in rapid succession, with the saw company and with the insurance company.

Here I was, with two strikes against me because of my record, turning down *two* jobs! I looked in the mirror and said, "Musgraves, you must be nuts!"

I thought I must be really cracking up when I found myself dialing George Donehower's phone number with the idea of asking him to reconsider me.

"As a matter of fact," he said after I'd told him why I'd called, "I *did* hire a guy."

"I was afraid of that," I murmured.

"Yeah, but, hold on, will you? He's not working out too good. Can you hold the line?"

He was back in about two minutes. "Musgraves? You're on. I just fired him."

It was a pretty good job, too. I operated the saw machine trimming metal and he let me adjust my work schedule to my school schedule. I'd go to classes till noon, then work from noon to eight or nine at night.

After that my time was my own. Or, rather, my family's and Christ's. Loris and I continued praying together, and teaching our children to pray and look for God's answer to our prayers.

Time flew. Then one Thursday evening at the Christian Center, after I'd finished my first semester at Southern California College, one of the pastors called me into his office. "Don, we've been looking over your grades for your first semester." He eyed me with a smile. "I don't know how you did it, working full time and going to school, too. You know what we decided? To accept your application for the Intern Program. You're in."

"Praise the Lord!" I cried. "When do I start?"

Talk about Cloud Nine! I had physically ached to get on the staff—to be involved in some way with the ministry at Melodyland Christian Center.

I now had to learn to minister to individual needs, to relate to people, to apply the Scriptures in a realistic fashion—not go off the deep end as I had at Loris' church.

Until I had found Jesus in the Orange County Jail, I had been playing roles, seeking identity. Now, I was lost in Jesus! I went around much of the time hardly aware of myself as a person at all, but rather as an instrument of the Holy Spirit.

Under any other circumstances, I'd have been run ragged with all the tasks that came my way, such as pinch-hitting for a Bible teacher, seeing people in mental or spiritual distress all over Orange County, and talking to people for hours trying to help them find a spiritual solution to problems.

Soon, I was teaching my own Bible class and going to evening meetings and prayer sessions whenever some emergency counselling appointment didn't pre-empt regular activities.

Presently, I was assigned to supervision of the prayer room. I'd work twelve to fourteen hours each Sunday there, and began to see some fantastic things.

I learned how to administer the Holy Spirit and instruct people in the Word so they could receive it. I learned how to teach them to let God heal them and fulfill their needs. I watched Jesus put families back together and heal children's speech and hearing problems.

I had started sharing the Holy Spirit with a group of fifteen ragtag, bearded, long-haired teenagers called the Chromatics. A lady named Mary Quintana, who had ministered most of her life in music, had volunteered to take these young people, who had started out with no natural talent for music but with a Spirit-filled drive to share Christ with others.

Mary taught them and they sang with a new beat young people could identify with. Regular old hymns and new songs both were adapted to real, toe-tapping music, lusty, bold, and full of the ecstasy of Jesus Christ and salvation.

I was really turned on by this group, particularly as I was still haunted by those screams of the dying kid in the Orange County Jail.

I was a dynamo, fired up by the Holy Spirit. And yet . . .

Yet . . . I still felt a longing.

While I made rapid progress in working with the Christian Center group, being a mere troubleshooter wasn't enough. I wanted to have a clearly defined ministry in which all my energies would be more concentrated. The Lord seemed to be nudging me impatiently.

I had such a strong desire for a ministry of my own that for days at a time I would fast and pray. I carried around Scriptures in my pocket to memorize. I'd pray in the Spirit and beg Jesus to make clear what He wanted me to do—what He was pushing me toward.

I was in the machine shop one day, so keyed up by my impatience to move faster and to understand God's intentions, I broke down and wept.

Then, the miracle happened! I had a vision!

I saw a pair of legs and feet. I could see where nails had been driven into those feet! Then, Jesus spoke to me—clearly, unmistakably: "Tell them I am going to raise up an army of young people. These young people will come from a life of discouragement. They'll want a place in our society."

I was awed. I sat there at my bench completely still, looking at those feet and listening to that soft voice.

"Tell them their training will be like a military situation, like the Green Berets," the Voice continued. "Those which I will train will be trained by being sent into 'enemy territory.' They will not know what they're going to do until they get there and receive their orders. They'll go into dangerous arenas, but not a hair on their heads will be harmed. Tell them they will do many exploits in my name. Tell them men will not pin medals on their chests, but they will be blessed in the Spirit. Their rewards will be what I give them."

A few days later I was scheduled to witness to Mary Quintana's group. When it was time for me to speak, I stood up, opened the Bible, started to give the Word —and the Lord spoke to me! "These are the ones," He said. "Tell them. They are the new army. . . ."

I forgot what I had planned to say; I had to share the vision. "Through my ministry and yours, God is going to raise an army," I said. "We will be as Christian soldiers, carrying the Word. . . ."

I was really fired up! The Holy Spirit fell on us all that night. They wept, prayed, and praised God. The Holy Spirit was so heavy for a while, I couldn't stand up.

This was to reconfirm the emphasis on youth at Christian Center. Christ's guiding hand was unmistakable in the events that followed.

One day, feeling I had to come out and specifically ask Jesus what He wanted me to do about the call He had given me, I decided to write down five things and then hold them up for the Lord to choose.

I prayed, "Lord, I want to be in your ministry. I know you have a place for me in one of these five situations.

Will you show me somehow where you want me?"

Friday night the telephone rang. It was George Wakeling, one of the men on Christian Center's newly formed youth Hotline Board of Directors, "Don, praise the Lord!"

"Yes, George," I said, "praise the Lord. How are you?"

"Fine. Listen, Don. The Director of the Hotline Telephone Ministry resigned today. I prayed about it and the Lord gave me your name to submit for Directorship. I . . ." He chuckled. "I want the job myself, but it's not time for me. So, I have just recommended your name to Pastor Wilkerson."

"You *what*? Never mind, I think I heard you," I said, stunned. How was it possible for the Lord to move so rapidly in answer to a prayer?

This, then, was the beginning of an activity to rescue a countless number of teenagers, and others, from sin, drugs, and suicide.

These events coincided with the negotiations by the Christian Center to take over the failing Melodyland Theatre in the round in Anaheim, across the street from the entrance to Disneyland. It looked like a huge, old-fashioned circus tent.

Christian Center, divided into five sections—worship, training, music, youth, and extension—had already used Melodyland's facilities, as well as those of the Anaheim Convention Center not far away, for the Dave Wilkerson Youth Rallies. (The two Wilkersons worked together and Ralph Wilkerson's Christian Center was the coordinating body for the youth rallies.)

I began my tasks as Director of the Melodyland Drug Prevention Center (MDPC) Hotline in one of the lobbies of the theater. The person who answered a call would rap with the caller to determine the problem and offer assistance.

The listener would also fill in whoever else was present so they could pray for the caller—or use another line to get the police rescue unit, an ambulance, or whatever.

I found myself glued to a telephone many hours every day, even though I delegated work to other volunteer workers, some of them members of the Chromatics music group. When I wasn't on the phone, I was running out

186

all hours of the day and night seeing people whose problems were urgent and desperate.

Talking with young people who were deep in drugs or had sexual hang-ups, on the one hand, and with community leaders and school officials, on the other, offering our cooperation in solving youth problems, I was learning fast. It was like taking a combination psychology and sociology course on the run.

While Director of the MDPC Hotline, I had many dramatic involvements with kids who were on the brink of disaster.

One night one of our girls answered the phone and gasped. She held her hand over the mouthpiece. "She's going to commit suicide!" She began to talk again with the caller while I grabbed the other phone.

"I've got a butcher knife," the girl on the other end said grimly. "I'm going to cut my throat. I thought pills would help me, but now it's worse than ever. Isn't any use going on."

I'm sure some of the callers would have gone through with suicide if we hadn't been there to literally tell them how Jesus and prayer could change their situation. We rapped with this girl for some time, then prayed her out of committing suicide. Today she is a Christian involved in the Melodyland youth outreach.

All the time I was learning how to help these people, figuring ways to approach them, learning to work on Christ's team at the Center—a team made up mostly of people who'd gone through the House of Horrors already—I was in a state I'd never known in my life. The more sordid and hopeless the situation, the more exuberant I was in slaying the dragons of drug and drink which Satan had sicked on so many young people.

By December of 1969, the MDPC not only operated the Hotline, but also handled "dope stop" lecture/discussion seminars at schools throughout Orange County, home information centers near schools where teenagers could get unbiased information on drugs, and provided speakers on the drug problem for service clubs and churches.

I also had to learn to relate to the school system. Dr. Bob Peterson, superintendent of the Orange County School District and a Christian, gave me the names of six people who could open doors to bring my seminar group into the schools. One of these was Lowell Jones, Curriculum Director of the Anaheim School District. A Christian, too, he was very excited about our proposed program.

We told these people we wanted our dope-stop team to share with teenagers the horrors and the healing our staff members had experienced when they were turned off drugs by Jesus Christ.

Three members of our team became very instrumental in keeping students off drugs. One of these was Donna Sturgill who had gotten involved with drugs just after finishing high school. Not long before her salvation, one of her friends, who had already blown his mind with acid, went the whole route and blew his head off with a double-barrelled shotgun. One night after a drug orgy in her home with a bunch of kids, she'd dropped some reds in her bathroom and later knelt at her bedside and prayed to God. He had revealed himself to her and she'd come to us to share her experience with us. Naturally, we put her to work.

Another staffer who shared his trials with the high schoolers was Gary Fisher. He'd spent fifteen years on drugs and had been in five mental institutions, where he'd had shock treatment. It took God, however, to overcome his problem, partly the result of alcoholic parents and a father who had tried to kill him with a butcher knife and a .22 rifle.

The third member of the team was Nanelle Fisher (now Gary's wife), who, at sixteen years of age, had been a pregnant heroin addict. She'd tried to kill herself four times, and the week before the Melodyland Drug Prevention Center became aware of her, she'd cut her wrists once again.

Donna, Gary, Nanelle, and I were soon speaking to an average of 10,000 teenagers a week. We hit one school a day for the whole school year, 125 schools in all that first year.

The main trouble we had was the school's fear of violating the Constitutional ban on religious groups on campuses. But we couldn't offer our Substitute for drugs without mentioning God because all we had to offer was Jesus Christ.

One high school principal was astonished at the miraculous way we'd penetrated the drug culture in his school. "I had given up trying to stop pot smoking in the rest rooms," he admitted. "But after your group got through with them . . . they're angels! What did you do?"

"Nothing," I answered. "Jesus did it."

One time Nanelle came back with the story of a fourteen-year-old girl who'd been forced to have sexual relations with her mother's boyfriend, who also happened to be a drug addict. The doper forced the girl to take drugs by threatening to harm her mother.

Nanelle and I promptly paid Mama a visit. Before getting out of our car, we prayed. God just had to help this poor girl! Otherwise, we were working for the wrong God. The mother invited us in and called her daughter. I looked around. No boyfriend!

We indulged in some small talk for five minutes; then I abruptly dropped the bombshell, telling her we knew the situation even if she didn't.

She broke down and cried—not in anger or belligerence, but in relief that someone had found out.

"We'd like to take your daughter out of this situation until you can get your own head on straight," I concluded.

The misguided mother agreed and the girl went to live for a while with Gary and Nanelle. Both mother and daughter later accepted Christ.

Another one of our challenges had its comic moments. Make a list of all the things you wouldn't want your own son to be. Then consider Ray Browning. He was effeminate, foul-mouthed, rebellious, and a guy whom the psychiatrists had given up after he'd been in and out of mental wards.

Very upset, Ray's sister contacted me one day. "Ray and Mom had a big fight," she panted. "He threatened to beat her up. Mom turned him in. He'd violated his probation, anyway."

There was another mom in this case, "Julia Jones," a lady who had volunteered to take in a kid who might need to "get away from it all." She was from the old-time

Pentecostal school, communicating God's love with a volume of hugs and kisses.

The problem for us was to get the judge to agree to ignore the probation violation and give Julia Jones a chance to do her stuff.

Sitting behind Julia as the judge considered this case, I became alarmed—she was beginning to shake and raise her hands. I thought, "Lord, if she raises her hands anymore in front of this judge, and starts to praise the Lord, we've had it. We'll never get Ray."

Shakily, I tapped her on the shoulder. "Cool it, Julia, I know what you want to do, and we appreciate your praying to God about this, but let's wait until we get Ray out of here."

We each had our chance to tell the judge our alternative for Ray, and evidently he thought it worth a trial. Ray was released in Mrs. Jones' custody.

This experience suggested another way we could be effective in salvaging young people from dope and destruction. We were getting so many phone calls from parents, wives, and addicts themselves, who were facing prosecution for drug offenses, that Gary and I began to frequent the juvenile courts, observing what was going on, speaking up for some teenagers who needed help not punishment.

Court officials began to release such kids to us. We'd find places for them to live where they would have a better chance to get their heads on straight in a wholesome, loving atmosphere. I took a few of these teenagers into my home. As far as Gary was concerned, he sometimes had them three deep in his apartment. George Wakeling had several living with him also.

Judges, police officers, and probation people were beginning to sit up and take notice! We discovered most officials were concerned about the people they have to deal with.

Two Anaheim policemen started coming to our Tuesday night meetings and got so excited, they took some of our outline cards to pass around to other officers. Patrol cars started coming into our parking lot to unload teenage dopers. Soon, all hours of the night the police were giving these teenagers a choice: hear our story or go to jail.

At this time, my office was a broom closet—small, with

room for two chairs and a desk. One morning I came into the canteen area next to my office, put the coffee on the hotplate, and went to my door. It wouldn't open. I pushed hard and finally got it open wide enough to see a teenager lying on the floor, saliva running out of his mouth, his eyes blood red and unfocussed, his speech that of someone stone drunk.

I moved him over and squeezed in. "What happened to you?" I asked.

"O.D., reds," he managed to groan.

I had just managed to get some coffee down him when another kid came in screaming about something after him. The all-night counselor helped me put him down, and we found he had dropped a tab of acid a few minutes before.

The day had just begun!

I had just enough time to find a place for these two to stay, when a girl rushed in with a .22 rifle in her hand. She looked like an Indian girl in a heavy jacket, levis, sweatshirt, and beads. She had short dark hair and a wild look in her brown eyes. She thrust the rifle at me, "Take this damn thing before I kill myself."

I grabbed the rifle, and talked with her a while. When she left I wondered what would happen to her.

The following Tuesday night, during our regular meeting, she was there. So were the two guys I had helped that day. The three of them made their commitments to the Lord!

Sylvia Martinez, one of our staff counselors, suddenly had a problem of her own. Danny, her son, was in Nellis Boys' School in Whittier. He'd been in institutions much of his young life.

One day Sylvia, looking distraught, said, "Danny's going to be released. I'm afraid he'll get into trouble again and go right back."

Gary and I advised her to "make him come to our program."

He came, all right. But it was for the girls.

Finally, our activities got to him. He was making some progress in getting to know the Lord when something threatened all his gains. Someone offended him on the way back from one of our singing trips. Danny was riding in a car behind us, and when we returned to the Melodyland parking lot, Danny was yelling and cursing another teenager.

They got out and confronted each other, about ready to let loose with fists. I walked over and stepped between them. "I know how badly you want to hit this guy, Danny," I said. "But, if it will do you any good, you can hit me instead." I paused, then added, "I won't hit you back. I want you to do this because I love you."

Staring at me as though I had doused him in cold water, he unclenched his fist, turned and walked away without another word. Later Sylvia said, "You know, Don, you're the only guy who's been able to help Danny. He knew you'd let him hit you, that you meant what you said."

"It wouldn't have mattered if he had," I replied. "I've been hit by bigger guys."

That wasn't the end of it. Another person came along to almost undo the good we'd done. And this one was a *deacon* in the church. He didn't care for long-haired hippies. He collared Danny and said, "Get your hair cut."

"Get lost, man," Danny retorted.

That did it. The man became enraged and started reading Danny the riot act. He used the strongest language a traditional Christian can.

Danny rushed out to the parking lot and broke a radio aerial off someone's car; he was going to whip the man.

The deacon, an ex-sheriff, always carried a revolver in his car. When we got out to the parking lot, we found the two of them squared off in the middle of the lot: Danny with the aerial in his hand, the deacon trying to get his revolver out of its holster—a long-haired teenager and an upstanding pillar of the church about to have their showdown. We calmed them down, but the deacon reported the incident to Pastor Ralph Wilkerson.

I figured the two insurgents had really blown it for the Drug Prevention Center's program of reaching out to these tough kids. I took Danny in to see Wilkerson, and Danny agreed to be counseled by him. By now he knew he'd been in the wrong. But I was sick about possible repercussions. The conservative faction of the church might disown us, even knowing what we were doing was vitally important. Somehow the gap between the traditional church and the needs of the people in the street had to be bridged.

After leaving Wilkerson's office, Danny and I spotted the deacon in the coffee room. I peered in and from the way he looked, I could tell God had dealt with him, too. He looked ready to bawl. Danny and I got to the back door of the Center and I said, "Danny, I don't know how you feel about it, but that old man in there—his heart is broken. He's realized how the whole thing looked— just as I do. And you. Listen, Danny." I touched his arm. "You've probably got more guts than he has. Why don't you go in there and say you're sorry? Do you have the guts to do that?"

Danny gulped. "Sure."

I watched that fifteen-year-old kid turn around and walk back to the coffee room. When I looked in, they had their arms around each other and were praising the Lord.

That was the beginning—the gulf between traditional Christianity and the street people disappearing.

Another boy who had a rough time *getting* up, then *staying* up, was Steve Sony. During a singing devotion, I noticed a very tall, nice-looking blond young fellow kneeling. I happened to catch his eye, and I don't think I've ever seen a stronger plea from anyone. I went to him and asked, "Steve, what do you want God to do for you?"

He just looked at me for a minute. Then, "I want Him to save me."

I put my hand on his head and started praying for him. The power of God came so strong it almost knocked Steve flat. If he hadn't already been on his knees, it would have thrown him to the floor. He wept and cried out to God. You could actually see God coming into his life!

He had just gotten himself straightened out, gotten off drugs, gotten a job, and bought a motorcycle, when he had an accident which banged up his arm. The doctor prescribed pain killers—*reds*—and gave him a bundle of them. He took a whole handful and the next thing *I* knew, I got a phone call at home.

Wishing I had a siren, I rushed to the Center and

got there in time to find Craig Rice, who has brain damage and is uncoordinated in his speech and walking, nevertheless walking with Steve around and around the church, trying to get him out of his stupor.

Saliva was dripping from Steve's mouth and he was blubbering. Stoned out of his mind. After talking to them briefly, I left Craig to go on walking Steve around, like a trainer exercising a horse.

Then Donna came running in. "Don! Don! They've got Steve and Craig surrounded on the other side of the building and are laying hands on him."

"What kind of hands?" I wondered. "Christian, or—?" I rushed out.

Twenty or thirty people were out there. One lady was emptying a bottle of vitamins into Steve's hands, and he was swallowing them so fast he almost choked. It suddenly dawned on me that it was Thursday and hundreds of staid church-goers were arriving for prayer meeting!

I explained the situation right there. I suggested if they wanted to help, that church members go inside and pray for Steve.

This scene wouldn't have happened if, when I'd first seen Craig and Steve outside, I'd remembered services were about to begin. It served the purpose, however, of introducing our work to these Christian Center church-goers, many of whom, though they'd heard about the Drug Center, had never seen it at work.

It was the best education they'd had in years.

Another difficult case that turned out to be one of our shinier examples was Bob Larson. He'd been well known in the Los Angeles area as a guitarist but had tripped out on marijuana and would often lose himself in semi-amnesia even while someone was talking to him.

This guy looked like a human toothpick. If he hadn't had on male clothing and a beard, I would have sworn he was a girl. He had beautiful long, blond hair. I took one look at him and said, "Oh, oh, here's one more that's going to cause a stir in our church." He'd come to the Center through the Chromatics musical group with whom I'd shared my vision. I felt the Lord was working through him and that God had made a call on him to preach. The Lord had started the ball rolling by delivering him from marijuana and getting him involved in the Hotline outreach.

Lack of funds constantly handicapped our efforts to save people from drugs and alcohol. Appeals for donations never brought in quite enough. Therefore, we presented our case to the public whenever possible.

One day Lowell Jones of the Anaheim schools wanted me to tell our story to the Rotary Club. When I got up to speak, I felt as though I were anointed. My talk came easily and with force. "My friend has given me five minutes to tell you what we need," I said. "It's as simple as this: I just left two teenagers in my office—teenagers who have overdosed on drugs and are now fighting to stay alive. We have the answer for their problem and for the troubles of thousands like them, but it takes money. We need funds to go on helping these people; frankly, I'm disturbed I had to leave these two guys to come over here to speak five minutes. We should be getting enough help not to have to take time out from our work to raise money. Nobody shows enough interest in what we're doing, and we can't seem to get enough publicity about our work, so no one is helping us in this way, either. Thank you very much."

I don't know how many men were touched, but I do know one was. He was Sam Campbell, editor of the *Anaheim Bulletin*. He sent a reporter, John Steinbacher, to see us the next day.

Those five minutes at the Anaheim Rotary Club put the Melodyland Drug Prevention Center on the religious map of the world, because Steinbacher's daily articles about the miracles that were taking place at the Hotline were the best public relations tool God could have created. We've used those articles over and over again.

The ripples from my little talk had grown into waves, spreading the word about our work. The Steinbacher articles in the *Bulletin* attracted the attention of Richard Dalrymple, a reporter of the Los Angeles *Herald Examiner*. When he interviewed me about the Center, I began to think something was amiss. He didn't seem to grasp what I was saying about the power of God to change lives.

Finally, he bluntly asked, "Can you explain what you mean?"

I spent the *next* half hour explaining to him what the Scriptures had to say about being born again, how the power of God comes in, how the Holy Spirit changes people's lives, and how He was changing kids' lives.

Dalrymple walked away, puzzled, shaking his head. I thought I'd failed to get the picture across. But at our next Tuesday night Hotline meeting, with about 700 people in attendance, whom do I see but Richard Dalrymple. And who was the first man to come down the aisle at the appropriate time for prayer? Richard Dalrymple.

He had been moved to a much deeper understanding of what he had been writing about—religion. Shortly thereafter he became religion editor of the *Herald Examiner.*

At this time we were going to take a Drugmobile around to shopping centers, and give out a drug paper to expand our outreach. While on this project, a man came from San Diego area and asked me to spend a few days telling his group about our activities.

There, at a youth conference, I met some new friends: Harold Brinkley, Director of Youth for Truth Ministry, of Sacramento; Mario Murillo, Director of Resurrection City, Berkeley; and Al Hopson, known far and wide as a black evangelist who has made a fantastic impact on college campuses and in Europe.

What a tremendous blessing it was for me because I was beginning to see God moving among the youth in a fantastic youth revival, especially on the West Coast.

I was amazed to discover that a big reason I'd been invited to talk to the youth conference was because our Anaheim Melodyland Drug Prevention Center had become a model for street counselling ministries in America. I was even more amazed to see our work had attracted the attention of *Look* magazine which published the world's first major article describing the Jesus People Movement.

It had been a long but good year. One of the joys of the new year was evaluating the gains we had made for God. One of these gains was the calming of a restless spirit by the name of Archie Strutt.

Archie had been one of the first men I'd counselled when I'd joined the Melodyland team. On the way out of a Thursday night meeting at Christian Center the previous year, where I had shared my prison experiences, Loris and I were startled by Archie walking toward me with an expression on his face as though he had gone beserk. I thought he was going to hit me. I stopped to see whether I was right or not. His teeth were clenched together in fury. He was angry because, during my testimony, I'd talked about being in jail.

He had just been released from Atascadero, Central California, where he'd been incarcerated. Shortly after having received the baptism in the Holy Spirit after twenty years in the Episcopalian church, he had lost control of himself one night. Because his church in all that time had never *really* mentioned the Lord in a true sense, he'd been so enraged he'd climbed to the roof of the church and cut off the cross.

I'd never met a guy with so much anger. My very words rekindled his hate and frustration. "Twenty years of my life wasted," he kept repeating over and over.

After talking with him, I agreed to counsel him and try to help him forgive, to use his enormous feeling for good. He became one of my first counselling subjects on a regular basis, coming to see me at home, my office, wherever we could get together. I spent many hours with him and began to see the Holy Spirit carry off the fury.

He became involved in our Wednesday evening prayer meetings and now, a year later, was soft-spoken. He'd received the baptism in the Holy Spirit at the Christian Center and now love, rather than anger, emmanated from him.

Riding high and busy doing the Lord's work effectively at last, introducing our Saviour to those who'd been fatherless so long in their atheistic hell, I couldn't understand why I kept feeling something—the Lord?—pulling me, pushing me, trying to *move* me away from all this.

"What is it, Lord?" I prayed. "Is this still not enough? Am I doing something wrong, after all?" I began to

197

feel unhappy, insecure, perhaps inadequate. I read Psalm 19 and I prayed, I prayed, I prayed.

Chapter 19

The blue-green water lapped over the sides of the car ferry and ran under the rented van packed with our household goods. Our Mercury station wagon was loaded with luggage, too, leaving just enough room for two children to stretch out.

We had been traveling for five days. It felt good to know we could stop driving for two hours.

The ferry nosed out of Port Angeles, Washington, early in the morning and headed across the Straits of Juan de Fuca. We could see the Olympic Mountains in the background of Port Angeles.

An unhappy feeling in my stomach added to the worry and uncertainty about our future. Out here in the middle of the Straits, I felt very small, helpless and humble. Everything was out of our hands now. We had made our decision to leave the United States and come to Canada.

Our biggest worry had been whether we could get into another country.

On deck Loris put her hand on my arm. "Don?" she hesitated. "Even though we're not sure of the future right now, I want you to know this has been the nicest trip I've ever had . . . with you and the children."

"Don't worry," I said. But I didn't feel confident. I was nervous, uneasy. It had happened again—the same thing that had happened before. I was shaky.

Now, as we stood on deck, the land looked far away. The next step we took would be in a different country.

"Daddy, Mommy, we're getting ready to dock," Lynne announced a half hour later. My reverie was cut short and the uneasy feeling returned.

"No wonder the land looked so far away," I said shakily. "I've been looking where we've been, not where we're going." I took Mike's hand and gave Loris a squeeze.

From Melodyland Hotline Center several months earlier, Loris and I had been called to go to San Diego. He made it known I was needed to start a hot line in an area filled with occult influences.

About one year previously, while I was still at Melodyland, Loris had received the baptism of the Holy Spirit one night when I had gone to San Diego to be a guest speaker. While I was talking, I had felt the strong presence of the Lord.

"It was just at that time," she confirmed. "I was sitting at the table in the kitchen reading the Bible. But I couldn't seem to understand anything. I closed it. I felt like singing. I started to sing but the words were different—like another language. Then I realized what was happening."

She grinned sheepishly. "I jumped up and closed the windows . . . like I used to do when you would get to praying so loud. The children had heard me and had come running to the kitchen. I told them what had happened. Then I took them into the living room with me and we all got down on our knees and prayed.

"It was just beautiful," she went on. "Oh, Don, do you remember I was always afraid I would get the baptism of the Holy Spirit in a way that would embarrass me? Well, I should have known better. The Lord seems to know how a person wants this . . . seems to know what is in each person's heart. Anyway," she went on, "I also received another message." She looked at me with a smile and her eyes shone. "They want you to come to San Diego to start another center, don't they?"

I felt so good I could hardly answer. "Well, that confirms it for sure, doesn't it?" I asked. At last. The Lord had told me to just let things be and He would see that my wife received the baptism of the Holy Spirit. He had been right, hadn't He? "Did He tell you that it was to be called the 'Action Center'?"

Loris laughed. "No, I didn't get all the details."

San Diego was my first experience in dealing with naked satanic power. The demonic activity was prevalent throughout the area we chose for a building, right on Pacific Beach. Our neighbors were three bars with drunks staggering by and a hippie leather shop. A Satanist motorcycle club met on the corner, and there was constant surfer traffic to and from the beach past our front door.

But, the Lord had told me this was the place. As soon as we opened the doors and put up the sign, in walked some of the beach traffic. "Where's the action?" asked one. He had long hair and dirty jeans, but he sported a brand new surfboard. Our sign read "Action Center," so I figured it was a logical question.

"Right here," I pointed to a broom and tools and lots of paint cans lined up against one wall. We hadn't even had time to sweep the place out.

He put down his surfboard carefully and picked up the broom. "Okay, man. I'll sweep." He turned out to be one of our first "volunteer crew members."

As the days went by, more kids wandered in, including a fourteen-year-old girl who'd been on pot and wanted to stay off. When we got those teenagers busy, it was amazing what they could do. Spirits were high, but so was Satan's power in that area.

During this time, we had all experienced the power of Satan, and we were anxious to show what the Lord could do. We had already had four converts and were looking forward to some big meetings.

One morning driving down Garnet Street to hit Mission Boulevard, my spirit was so closed I felt as if I could hear the demons screaming.

The night before, after one of our meetings when nothing had happened (not one person had come forward), I kept thinking about those jeering faces around the fire we had built on the beach. An anointing had come over me to pray. It was such a fierce thing that I woke up, got out of bed and was down on my knees while still half asleep.

By the time I got to Mission Boulevard I knew I was free. The Center was free, too: demonic activity was bound! From that time on our Tuesday and Saturday night teenagers were starting to be delivered by the Holy Spirit.

Other miracles were beginning to happen, even with the inexperienced volunteer counselors manning the phones. We had an "on the spot" training program and worked as quickly as we could, training people as soon as they were capable of handling even the smallest job. When someone picked up a phone, they never knew what was going to be on the other end, but these kids were filled with the Holy Spirit; He was telling us what to do.

Things were beginning to go smoothly at the Center when we received some adverse publicity in one of the local newspapers. A long article had been written about us because someone had asked a columnist about our organization and what we had to offer. He had had several friends and acquaintances call our staff when we had first opened. To some who were not familiar with our operation, it might have seemed as if they got the wrong advice. In the article we were raked over the coals for not having any Ph.D.s or trained social workers on our staff. We knew the writers hadn't even come down to the Center.

Dave Balsiger, a journalist working with us at the Center, suggested I invite him down. I did, and he accepted.

After talking with him for fifteen minutes, I realized his sole purpose in coming had been for more ammunition for his column. I told him about some of the members on our staff, and how they had already helped both themselves and other young people—on drugs. I outlined the whole hot-line program from its conception in Anaheim. I didn't seem to be getting anywhere. Then I started telling him about some of our recent converts.

"At one of our meetings on the beach the other night," I said, "I noticed a girl who looked unhappy. Worse, she actually looked tormented. I watched her and said a prayer for her, over and over. I didn't forget her face. A few days later she came into the Action Center. She told me what was bothering her. She said she was afraid of her own father because he forced her to have sexual relations with him every opportunity he got. She said she couldn't sleep anymore because she was always afraid he would come into her room."

I could see that this was making an impression. "This girl and I prayed together right in the office, and she could see that there was still hope. Then after repeated calls by me and some of the members of our staff, and with the help of the Juvenile Probation Department, we got her father to accept psychiatric treatment. (He wouldn't accept ours!) Judy accepted the Lord and she is now back in school, a much happier girl. She'll probably join our staff someday, but right now we are encouraging her to 'grow up' at a normal pace."

"You mean you call on other agencies, too?" he asked.

Now we're getting somewhere, I thought. "Yes, but they don't always have the right answers, either. Take the case of the girl who had just been released from the hospital. She had been there for ten days, going through withdrawal. They had recommended that she be put on methadone, but she was afraid this wouldn't help, just put her right back on something else. She came to *us* for help."

"What could you do for her that the medical profession couldn't?"

"Well," I went on. "I didn't spend a lot of time in dialogue. By the look on her face, she was desperate. When I talked with her about God doing a miracle, she knew unless He *did* give her a miracle, there was no hope. I laid my hands on her and asked God to heal her. The power of God came over her, she began to weep and thank God for coming into her life. In the next few weeks, we found a young lady who could make it—and a new counselor! We hope to have her on one of our radio programs concerning drug abuse."

He still looked skeptical. We had been talking for forty-five minutes. Suddenly, the Lord impressed me to ask him to be on our board of directors. I knew his background and I knew he was interested in drug abuse. When I asked him, his attitude changed immediately.

"You see, I'm head of a Drug Abuse Program sponsored by the Community Health Center here. We set up a classroom situation and train counselors in relating to kids. Look, I'm sorry, I didn't realize there were other ways to do this."

Then he began to tell *me* about all the other commitments he had. I knew now why the Lord had sent him to me. In the next ten minutes he began telling me about his life and all the problems he had.

"You may think it strange, but we believe God will take a hand in a person's life if you ask Him," I said. "That is why we're here. We can take these drug-abuse problems and put them right into the hands of Jesus Christ." He was fidgeting in his chair. "Would it offend you if I prayed for you?" I asked.

"No," he answered quickly.

I prayed for him and the power of God was so strong in that room, he could hardly get out of his chair. He thanked me profusely and literally staggered to his car *under the power of God!*

His next article praised the Action Center—almost overdoing it.

Then unexpectedly, like a thunderbolt, the Lord started to tell Loris and me that we were to move on again!

"Lord, what now?" I asked that night in prayer. "We just got settled and I wouldn't even know who to appoint to run the place!" As I said this, a name came to mind: Bob Larson. He had been working with us at the Action Center and he was already two and a half years old in the Lord. I knew he hadn't had such responsibility as this.

The next day I called him into my office. "Bob, if I have to leave and go to another ministry soon, do you think you could take over Action Center?"

He stared at me in disbelief. Then he responded as I had hoped he would. "I'll pray about it, Don," he had said.

Another month went by; we still hadn't received any kind of a sign telling us where we should go.

Harald Bredesen, one of the earliest leaders of the current Charismatic Renewal, turned out to have the answer. It was suggested by a friend that I write to him regarding the Lord's current leading on my situation. "I think he's got a ministry going up in Canada now," my friend said. "Possibly he needs help there."

Loris and I began to pray about Canada. Then I met Mr. Bredesen at a conference in Ventura, California, and we were in perfect harmony with each other from the start. He was enthusiastic about a church in Canada, on Vancouver Island. "They sure could use a hot line up there, Don. And some help in turning those kids the right way. It sounds as if you're the man the Lord is going to send."

But I felt I needed scriptural confirmation of God's desire for us to go. Lying awake at two o'clock in the morning, I began to pray. I got up and looked out at the street lights. Joshua 1:3 came to mind. "Every place that the sole of your foot will tread upon I have given to you as I promised Moses."

That was it. That was all I needed.

Loris received confirmation from Hebrew 11:8, 9 that same night: "By faith Abraham, when he was called to go out into a place which he should after receive for an inheritance, obeyed; and he went out, not knowing whither he went. By faith he sojourned in the land of promise, as in a strange country, dwelling in tabernacles with Isaac and Jacob, the heirs with him of the same promise."

"And that's enough for me, Don," she said. Daily we prayed about it. Then an invitation came from the church in Canada.

"This will be a real 'faith walk,' " I told Loris.

I called Bob in again. "It looks as though the time has come, Bob. The Lord has shown us we are to go to Canada. I'll recommend you for Director of the Action Center."

"I've been praying about it since you told me," he said. "It looks as if that's what He wants, too."

"Daddy, the man is signalling for you to move up!" Mike said.

"Oh, yeah." I shifted gears and pulled up, reaching for my papers.

The Immigration Official looked at them briefly, then said, "I'm sorry, it looks as if there's been some mistake. Pull over to the side and have your wife do the same. I'll meet you in the office."

I pulled over and motioned for Loris to follow.

He checked our papers. "Someone has given you the wrong information. Frankly, we can't allow you to come into our country. I'm going to have to deport you."

"But, sir," I said. "If it will help any, I have a letter that shows we're invited to come to Canada to work. I was told this was all that was necessary: a guaranteed income, or a job."

"Well," he suggested, "why don't you and your family go and have some lunch on a free pass and look around a bit. I'd like to have you talk with the supervisor, and he won't be back here until two o'clock."

We walked up to the town, but it was hard to enjoy Victoria's beauty.

"Daddy, are we going to get to stay?" the children asked.

"I don't know. It's in the hands of the Lord, now." I breathed a silent prayer to Him. "If it be your will . . ."

The supervisor was waiting for us. Briefly I told him our story, giving him some of my testimony. He was more sympathetic than I expected but still adamant. The law says anyone convicted of a crime cannot enter this country.

"I can give you two alternatives," he said, "Go back of your own free will at your expense or we'll have to deport you. But it will be on the records, yours, your wife's and even the children's, that you've been deported."

I turned to Loris. "It doesn't look as we have much choice, does it?" She shook her head. "Do you mind if I call the church and tell them what has happened?"

A church elder, Mr. Stone, who was an attorney, came down to talk with us. He was perturbed but said, "I feel helpless. There isn't much I can do on such short notice. We'll have to check further and let you know."

"We'll go back to Port Angeles and call you from there tomorrow morning," I suggested.

By the time we got back to Port Angeles and found a motel for the night, we had been traveling for more than fifteen hours. We just dropped to our knees and prayed.

The next morning we called Dr. Stone. "I still don't know what to tell you, Don," he answered. "It seems you shouldn't have been granted anything until they had checked it through Ottawa. It doesn't look too promising."

"We'll go back to Seattle, then," I told Dr. Stone. The Lord had ministered to me to say that. He seemed to be guiding me again. "Thanks for all of your help. We'll let you know where we're staying as soon as we find a place." I knew we had just enough money to get back, pay for the truck, get a motel, and then find a place to live.

By now, I was beginning to suspect we wouldn't get to Canada at all. It was a real blow. Up to this point, all my "messages" from the Lord had seemed to be correct. All systems had been go. This was a major setback. To come all this way—spend all our money—then . . . fizzle!'

But by the time we got to Seattle, my spirits had risen. "Everyone on the lookout for a decent looking motel, but no swimming pool!" I warned. "We won't be here long because we're going to find a place to live—today! God, you're just going to have to work another miracle," I said out loud.

Neither one of us knew anything about Seattle, but Loris and I started going through the house ads as soon as we found a motel. I put my finger on one at random. It was a three-bedroom house and the rent fit our pocketbook. I telephoned, talked to a complete stranger and told him our plight.

"Well, praise the Lord!" he answered. "I'm John Nelson and the Lord must have sent you. Come on over."

John Nelson turned out to be our miracle. We rented the house, unpacked, and went out into the backyard to pray. Nelson joined us. He was of Lutheran background and, as we found out later, was hungry for the baptism of the Holy Spirit. He and his wife both later received the baptism of the Holy Spirit. He was so glad to share with someone that he practically laid out the red carpet.

When we went back for the truck, suddenly there

were many hands to help. The neighborhood was full of children of all ages and they pitched in and helped.

A welcome by the mayor himself couldn't have made us feel better. We invited them to come back the next day, and our children began to learn what it is to minister to other children.

The girls set up song-fests and had Bible readings, Mike had prayers. Several of the children accepted the Lord. This was a great boost to us all.

At the suggestion of Dr. Stone, Loris and I talked to the Immigration Office and found that if we had letters of recommendation vouching for my rehabilitation, it might help my case. "You'll need about eleven or twelve," they said.

"Well, that'll be easy," I told Loris. I telephoned Melodyland Christian Center and asked them to help me out. Then we waited.

But something was wrong. Neither Loris nor I had the feeling the Lord really wanted us to go to Canada.

While we waited for the letters, Harald Bredesen told me I ought to see Dick Simmons. "He has a representative in Vancouver, Canada." Simmons had something to do with job therapy for prisoners. A letter from him might mean something to the Immigration Authorities.

"We'll see," I told Loris. "Letter or no, I'd like to meet him and talk with him about job therapy. Maybe God has led us to him for a reason."

Chapter 20

The minute I met Dick Simmons, I recognized a spiritual affinity. It was one of those crazy things that can't be all coincidence—a meeting planned by the Lord. As we got to talking, I mentioned that *The Cross and the Switchblade* had been of prime importance in my salvation. The strangest look came into Simmons' eyes. "I was Dave Wilkerson's assistant director—actually running Teen Challenge—while he was busy with that book!" he exclaimed.

Simmons had been a Presbyterian minister in New York's ghettos who had helped Dave make inroads for Jesus among street gangs.

In the 1960s, he'd moved to Washington and, in 1965, helped set up Job Therapy, Inc. The idea was to match up volunteers in the "free world" with prison inmates who expected to be released within a year. Volunteers were screened for their responsibility, emotional stability, and ability to relate. They visited their "match" at least once a month, helped them line up a job, spent the first day with them and continued to help while the ex-con was getting adjusted.

"So many people in institutions have no one," Simmons pointed out. "No one visits them. No one writes to them. No one *cares*. Job Therapy provides that *someone*. It's like giving a guy a substitute father. Eighty-five percent of the inmates in state prisons are fatherless, never had a dad to relate to."

I had the impression God had given Simmons a message that He cared for the fatherless and expected His sons to share this joy of caring for the lost. "Pure religion and undefiled before God and the Father is this," says James 1:27, "to visit the fatherless and widows in their afflictions, and to keep himself unspotted from this world."

Now a piece of the puzzle had been filled in: why God had had Loris and me come to the Northwest. He wanted us to be impressed with the need of the lost to be fathered by the saved. Now I knew the Lord had been leading me to involvement in ministering to men in prisons.

Ezekiel says God judged Sodom and Gommorah, not only because they were so wicked and perverted, but because their citizens failed to help the fatherless and poor.

Simmons reinforced the idea. I'd said upon meeting him, I thought God had led me to Canada. "I don't think so," he'd responded. "I think He led you to me."

As Loris and I sojourned in Seattle, becoming acquainted with Job Therapy and the staff, it became clearer that the Lord wanted me to increase my skills in dealing with all those concerned in this type of ministry: inmates, authorities, placement people, church members from whom were drawn volunteers to help.

"Most of the fifty men on the Job Therapy staff," Simmons told me, "are trained and experienced; however . . ." He looked at me for a moment, as if again struck by the feeling I'd been sent. "Not too many have had much experience with drugs and how to relate to users. Your work at Melodyland put you in contact with drug users. If you worked with us, you could contribute that experience and, at the same time, learn more about dealing with people in prison."

I told Simmons I would pray about it to determine God's will. He invited me to observe activities at Job Therapy headquarters and become acquainted with the staff. Frequently, I attended morning prayer session which opened each new day at JT headquarters.

Through observation and study, I began to learn the meaning of helping the fatherless. I re-read scriptures referring to the fatherless. Deuteronomy 10:18-19 was an especially good general example of the Bible's exhortations to help others: "He doth execute the judgment of the fatherless and widow, and loveth the stranger, in giving him food and raiment. Love ye, therefore, the stranger: for ye were strangers in the land of Egypt."

I could point out to the prospective Job Therapy volunteers how they are blessed for such help, as Job was blessed because he took the position and cause of those he did not know—actually searched them out to help them, as described in Job 29:11-16: "When the ear heard me, then it blessed me; and when the eye saw me, it gave witness to me: because I delivered the poor that cried, and the fatherless and him that had none to help him. The blessing of him that was ready to perish came upon me; and I caused the widow's heart to sing for joy. I put on righteousness, and it clothed me: my judgment was as a robe and a diadem. I was eyes to the blind, and feet was I to the lame. I was a father to the poor: and the cause which I knew not I searched out."

The Lord's blessings on those who do this work is also assured in Matthew 25:40, "And the King will answer them, 'Truly, I say to you, as you did it to one of the least of these my brethren, you did it to me!' "

Studying Scriptures, I saw that along with merely lining up jobs for inmates, people were needed who would implement God's blessings on the fatherless, help them to be delivered from their problems by the supernatural power of the Holy Spirit.

It was ironic. The more I amassed evidence, the more I found the very two things which would seem to have been my most significant contributions to Simmons' group were those which ultimately affected my decision *not* to join the staff on Job Therapy in Seattle. Surely the Lord had *not* led me to Dick Simmons for a permanent association, but rather the initial motivation for my work.

Restless and wanting to be useful to the Lord, I helped a man, Mike Maloon, start a hot line, which he called Seattle's Highest High. Mike's home was available, and he had already secured a telephone number. I helped him promote it and solicit church groups to participate and support it.

Despite the good I was doing in this respect, I did not feel the Lord intended me to take a major part in maintaining this hot line.

God's hand was more evident, however, in creating

an opportunity to make further contacts, and gain further insights, in the next few weeks. For Dick Simmons and I were enabled to embark on a witnessing-learning tour which enriched me in Christian work among prison inmates.

During the tour, I lost track of time. It was a whirlwind trip that included meetings, conferences, and testimonies at churches, and covered the entire Pacific coast from Oregon to Southern California.

We listened to an address by Lou Nelson, warden of San Quentin, who was speaking to a conference of the correctional institutions of Oregon.

Nelson impressed me with his honesty and straightforwardness. He'd been sought as a guest speaker because he had excellent control of his prison, yet was in charge of one of the roughest in the United States. He was a man who dealt with inmates with an iron hand, yet with an honest evaluation of, and genuine concern for, the welfare and needs of the men under his care.

After the meeting, I looked him in the face as he stood in the empty auditorium talking to another man.

"I really appreciate you," I said.

We talked, and he showed an understanding of my feelings about the fatherless, the need to bring Christian comradship to inmates.

When he was a young man, he told me, he had been tempted to go along with a gang's plans to knock over a liquor store. "But my father had been converted a few years previously, and, as I thought about what this bunch of hoods were going to do, I kept hearing my father's voice, saying, 'God will punish you.'"

It was having such a father as he had had, he said, that had made the difference in his life.

In later talks, he drove home the fact that society fails the correctional institutions.

"This is your institution," he said to a group of Christians at one meeting; meaning *all* of ours. "You built it and send men to it. The prison takes the failures society produces, and after the correctional institution has finished with these people, society fails to help rehabilitate them. No one helps them re-enter the free world, find jobs and places in the community. Employers won't hire them; there is no provision for offering ex-cons guidance.

"Parolees need to feel they are accepted as rehabilitated. They feel they have served their time and resent the continuous punishment long after they have paid for their offenses. Punishment should be followed by a period of loving and acceptance, with the institutions supplying the punishment, society providing the rewards. There's no one but you who can effect this."

When Simmons and I visited Job Therapy in Oakland, California, I became acquainted with Roger Duerksen, who was chairman of the board. JT California expected soon to sign contracts with four different California correctional institutions—San Quentin, Folsom, Duel at Tracy and the hospital at Vacaville. The institutions were to allow selected JT volunteers to visit. This new group had substantial help from federal financing.

Duerksen heard me witnessing to a church group in Sacramento, sharing what had happened to me and about the concept of the fatherless. Afterwards he looked at me as though he were in a state of shock. "That was amazing," he finally said. "A really moving testimony."

Back in Seattle, I received a call from Will Rose of Job Therapy in Oakland. "I've been talking with Roger Duerksen," Rose said. "We've decided to ask you to join our staff here."

"*Move*?" Loris said, blinking, when I dropped the bombshell. "But . . . but . . . but . . . !" She took a deep breath and started over again. "Where? To Canada? Alaska? Thailand?"

"California," I replied.

"But we just came from there!"

I explained the situation, with some difficulty. How *do* you explain something like this, especially when you don't understand it yourself?

"But the children don't get out of school for another six weeks," she protested.

"I'll just have to go down ahead. You and the kids can join me when school's out."

I did just that, though reluctantly, with the sad feeling

that, once again, I was to be separated from my family. The six weeks passed slowly; but finally, Loris and the children joined me and we set up housekeeping in Hayward, near Oakland.

The next *eight months* was like living in a whirlwind.

My job was largely a selling one—selling denominational people on the need to help men released from institutions to go straight. I explained our "M-2"—Man-to-Man—philosophy of Job Therapy California to groups and individuals. I had to try to make people see life from parolees' viewpoint.

I had to explain that for someone who has been behind bars for a long time, his first few weeks in the free world can be psychologically chaotic. Everything looks different: street corners, cars, just walking along the street has to be re-learned. It's kind of Rip Van Winkle awakening, where once-familiar scenes seem strange and forbidding.

After several years, ex-cons develop an aversion to standing in lines. One man who'd gone to get his driver's license was almost a basket case by the time he got up to the window. He couldn't take the driver's test. If he'd had someone to go with him, he might have made it.

In the Oakland job therapy programs the volunteer accompanies the ex-inmate everywhere on his first day out. He's like an escort, or tourist guide. He makes himself available afterwards whenever the parolee needs advice or just companionship.

The volunteer sometimes changes more than the man he re-introduces into the world. Deriving new insights into others' troubles can be very educational!

Simmons had pointed out that it is not the job of the volunteer to rehabilitate the man, but rather to help him rehabilitate himself. It's a motivational and inspirational function, giving the man a sense that he is still a *person*.

Bill Bates was one of the volunteers. He had learned about the program through an orientation meeting. When the time came to go to the prison to visit his new friend, he became very apprehensive.

"Usually," he reported, "I don't have trouble meeting new people. I received Frank's letter the day before

Easter, from San Quentin, duly censored, of course, with his picture, background information, etc. I fought a strong temptation to put off going through with that first visit!

"When I woke up the next day, the day I was supposed to visit him, however, I had the impulse to go right up there *first*, on my way to church for Easter services, instead of later, as scheduled. I don't know where this impulse came from. When I got to the prison, my new friend's attitude showed me I needn't have worried.

"Man, he was so happy to see me he was actually bubbling. He was really excited. He talked for an hour and I tried to be a good listener. He couldn't contain himself! He burst with enthusiasm. When they'd called his name on the loudspeakers while he was still out in the yard, he couldn't believe his ears.

"On the second visit, he said, 'The first time *I* was talking so much about myself that I didn't find out much about you. Mind if we talk about *you* this time?'

"I laughed. 'Of course not,' I said. I told him a lot about myself, and I was surprised at the way so many things I take for granted were such a revelation to him."

Later Bates received a letter from him:

Hi Bill,

If the postman don't strike or if the government doesn't devalue the stamp, or your mail box isn't ripped off, you might receive this letter. Bill Bates, you don't appear to be a Bill Bates but then again I do hope you'll overlook my questioning and suspicious attitude.

It's from conditioning rather than habit. Okay, Bill, I do need a friend. It is hell trying to plough through humanity and it's more important my need to give and share and relate and communicate. . . .

Would you believe some of the things you take for granted I have never known? I've never had a driver's license, never owned a car, or had a bank account.

Geez! I never even had a friend. I'm 36 years old and haven't been in the free world more than a year at a time since I was a teenager. I think—rather, I *know*—I'm ready to handle this now. Thanks for listening. See you Saturday.

Sincerely,
Frank

The average person is surprised that many men in

institutions do not even know how to open a bank account or write checks.

Many, indeed, have never known a friend. They are the fatherless. Perhaps it was because they didn't know how to *be* a friend.

Many of these guys don't know how to be *grateful.* They were never taught how to be.

Besides explaining the program to Christian people, I also had to sell employers on the desirability and practicality of hiring people who have been in jail, some of whom had received valuable job training while serving time.

For me it was a learning situation. I had had a prison background, I had dealt with dopers, and I had a real burning desire to bring Christ into the hearts of those with whom I talked. Now I was adding the ability to negotiate with down-to-earth, everyday people who were accustomed to dealing with employment situations in a routine way. I had to convince them that the traditional reluctance to hire ex-cons was short-sighted, narrow-minded, fallacious, incorrect, and unChristian.

I had to soft-pedal this latter. I was learning to curb my enthusiasm, and at the same time plant seeds which might bear fruit later.

It is easy for the affluent to send donations to foreign missions, or give money to be administered by some unseen high church body. This is needed, too, of course. But it's hard to get people to share *themselves* with those in need, to give a few hours to someone who has nothing but time—the wrong kind of time.

At church groups many times, I passionately pleaded with people to hearken to Scripture on this matter, to hearken, for example, to Isaiah 1:16-17: "Wash yourselves; make yourselves clean; remove the evil of your doings from before my eyes; cease to do evil; learn to do good; seek justice, correct oppression; defend the fatherless, plead for the widow."

If you tell them the story, you can involve people in working with the fatherless. Just as with so many of the fatherless in prisons who haven't been taught, nobody *has* been talking to free people about the responsibility Christians have.

During the eight months of "on the job training in Job Therapy," I learned, too, that correctional officials *are* eager to learn new ways of reaching the men and changing them.

The prison *system* unfortunately obscures the basic desire of most prison officials to do the job they are supposed to do: rehabilitate lawbreakers. Reform is held back by a lack of proper financing, misconceptions, ignorance, and unwillingness to invest large initial sums of money.

Millions of dollars are spent annually to maintain the present system, but it's spread out and doesn't appear so obvious as would a still larger lump sum paid out for reform, even though such an initial investment would dramatically reduce the steady, year-by-year outlay of money to support the existing system.

The division of church and state also handicaps prison officials who try to effect changes. Whether from their own personal belief, or because of policies laid down from above, they have resigned themselves to "tried-and-true," conservative, easily regulated, and strictly controlled religious activities in prisons.

Fear, stemming from lack of knowledge and conviction, keeps out the "noisier" chaplains and volunteer pastors who vibrate with God's joyful Spirit.

Having learned to use more subtle ways of testifying to those whose hearts were not prepared, I had become careful not to frighten people off with my own exuberance.

More and more the Lord spoke to me, telling me my time here was coming to an end, that I had just about fulfilled my mission. The feeling nagged especially during the month of June, 1972, so once again the same old story repeated itself: bringing something to birth, then moving on.

Was it God who planted in me a fantastically strong urge to return to Southern California, and work in association with Melodyland Christian Center!

Melodyland, indeed, seemed to be the center of a revival to minister to institutions, according to correspondence I had with people on the scene. I wanted to be a part of that!

I went south to see Melodyland Pastor Ralph Wilkerson. I told him how I felt. I shared my idea that the Lord wanted me back in Anaheim.

We talked for a while then, praise the Lord, the Holy Spirit moved on both of us. It was almost visible, something we could hear, touch. We realized God was confirming my hunch.

When I returned to Oakland to conclude my stay at Job Therapy, I had for the first time in several months such a feeling of being in the will of God that it was a blessing for everyone, inspiring those around me—not through my own acts but through the Holy Spirit shining through.

Chapter 21

"Step right up, ladies and gentlemen, boys and girls. See the greatest show on earth: God's will performed daily and nightly. It doesn't cost a thing. Except your life. Just one life, folks—donated to Jesus Christ. Step right *up* . . ."

As I sit at the desk in my Southern California Chrisma Ministries office, I automatically think in terms of the verve and gaiety of the circus and of compelling music that catches the heart, for such images are symbolic of the New Christianity, a Christianity that has replaced gravity with joy abounding.

We still believe in the agonies of hell, but heaven is no longer so far away. We believe God gives us happiness right here on earth if we but accept His Son, Jesus Christ, and allow ourselves to be infused with the blessings of the Holy Spirit. God is love, peace, and joy, in the face of the taunting, tempting world around us.

As President of Chrisma Ministries my duties are intermingled with the ministries of the Melodyland Hotline Center. At the Hotline the kinds of problems helped are legion—all of those caused by drugs, alcohol, sex, occult involvement, and crime.

The ten local telephone lines and the national WATS toll free counseling lines are lit up 24 hours a day—7,000 calls a month. The volunteer staff has grown from five to seventy-five plus a full-time staff of twenty-seven young adults and teenagers. Seven different music groups perform at churches, prisons, and hospitals, even on the streets, in catchy songs that lift hearts to Christ.

At a regular Tuesday night meeting held by the Melody-land Hotline Center, perhaps up to 1,500 former dopers, ex-cons, and just plain, ordinary people learn about the hope we hold out through Jesus Christ to bring light into dark lives.

Through the contacts and experience I have gained over the past two years, I have formed definite ideas on how prisons can more effectively rehabilitate those sent to them by the courts.

It is heartwarming to note a trend toward smaller correctional units located in the community rather than the large warehousing of multitudes of men separated from society. Imprisoned closer to their families, inmates have a better chance to retain family ties, are more encouraged to "go straight" once they are free. Families can visit inmates, help make them feel they are still *wanted* by them.

Another change which is taking place more slowly but which I believe of equal importance in reducing prison size, is bringing inmates and mates together for regular conjugal visits. This practice has proven highly successful in some areas, giving inmates incentive for "good behavior." The practice reduces family split-ups, reduces the homosexual problem in prisons.

Some institutions allow prisoners weekend furloughs to be with their families. Some allow less serious offenders to work during the week.

All the proposed changes in the rehabilitation process cannot be completely successful and effective without that ingredient which feeds the spiritual hunger of the inmate, a hunger he may not recognize but which is in all of us: the infusion of the Holy Spirit.

Until people in and out of jails, prisons, and mental hospitals do acknowledge the importance of Christ in *lives*, recurring problems will mar the most skillfully designed program.

For this reason, a major revolution in the spiritual atmosphere in institutions is of utmost importance. Chaplains, hired under restrictive civil service regulations, and so overworked that they cannot reach the total institutional population, are unable to do the entire job.

Correctional authorities must seriously consider admitting volunteer Christian teams to prisons and giving them a proper degree of freedom to bring Christ into the hearts of the fatherless.

Christian teams are needed in mental hospitals, too, where often patients seldom see overworked doctors and counsellors. Such teams can offer spiritual therapy. In the majority of mental abberration, according to our view, mental illness is very often due to demonic oppression.

As I sit in my Chrisma Ministries office in Orange, considering some of these thoughts, I am pleased that I have already had a part in opening a number of prison doors to increased visitations, not only to inmates' friends and relatives and new friends who father the fatherless, but also to Christ in the cells where previously only the profane outpourings of Satan have been heard.

Jesus sent His disciples out in *groups*, and we all know that "in union there is strength." Witnessing teams, having persuaded officials to admit them, go on to bring comradeship, Christ, and cheer into lives virtually forfeited to Satan.

Just before winding up affairs with Job Therapy in Oakland, I had the opportunity to take over a class in creative dynamics at San Quentin.

During the classes, I told my story, describing the creative power of God in reshaping my wretched life. As I shared with inmates my own experiences, I brought in the fact that all the groups working in prison situations, like Alcoholics Anonymous or Yoke Fellows, have a step that is called the Fifth Step, where people share their feelings—put their worst foot forward.

As we talked, I noted the faces and the responses of the men who identified with me when I talked of being an imposter, playing roles, reaching out for an identity that was always out of reach—until I'd found Christ.

"Acknowledging what you are, helps you see what

you've been," I told them. "The Bible itself suggests getting things out in the open, where you can look at them and see what pieces have made the puzzle that is *you*."

Before classes were concluded, some of the guys began to realize that unless they got honest with themselves, they didn't have much of a chance.

The ultimate purpose of the class was to show the men that they were responsible for what they had done, and to destroy the rationalization they'd used to excuse their conduct.

That evening when I was leaving, passing through the Big Yard overlooked by the tiers of cell blocks, the hum and drone of voices in the clear air seemed to start vibrations within me.

As I walked toward the gate I prayed that I might have left these men something that would change their lives.

Driving over the long Golden Gate Bridge, I wasn't aware of time, or of the lights of the cities around the bay on the dark waters. God was speaking to me!

He said I would develop a ministry acceptable to correctional people. I would evolve a ministry related to prisoners showing them how to receive Jesus Christ. And He would help me develop a team that would be professionally successful at creating job opportunities for the fatherless, and counseling for their wives and children.

He would provide, clear across the nation, Christian people who would respond to the message to visit inmates who have been forgotten.

I prayed many times with great fervor that this vision would be fulfilled. I am happy to say that this man, who had dipped into the dark waters of hell itself to find *Him*, has a part *in* this prophecy to help it come true.

Any reader requests, comments, or inquiries for speaking engagements should be directed to:

Don Musgraves
Chrisma Ministries
P.O. Box 5992
Orange, CA. 92667

Appendix I

The following are prison ministries offering information or participation opportunities.

Chrisma Ministries
P.O. Box 5992
Orange, Calif. 92667

Job Therapy
1558 "B" St.
Hayward, Calif. 94541

Job Therapy
150 John St.
Seattle, Wash. 98010

The Shepherd Foundation
P.O. Box 141
Lynwood, Calif. 90262

Institutional Division
Melodyland Hotline Center
P.O. Box 999
Anaheim, Calif. 92805

Appendix II

Additional Recommended Reading

1. Joy Adams, *Competent to Counsel*, Baker Book House, Grand Rapids, Mich.
2. Paul E. Little, *How to Give Away Your Faith*, Inter-Varsity Press, Downers Grove, Ill. 60515
3. Henry Blocker, *Suicide*, Inter-Varsity Press, Downers Grove, Ill. 60515
4. Francis A. Schaeffer, *He Is There and He Is Not Silent*, Tyndale House, Wheaton, Ill.
5. Anonymous, *Go Ask Alice*, Prentice Hall, Englewood Cliffs, N.J.
6. Phil Thatcher, *Under Arrest*, Shepherd Foundation, P.O. Box 141, Lynwood, Calif. 90262
7. Jerry Dunn, *God Is for the Alcoholic*, Pyramid Books, New York, N.Y.
8. Byron Eshelman, *Death Row Chaplain*, Prentice Hall, Inc., Englewood Cliffs, N.J.